A REBEL'S RIDE TO REDEMPTION

A REBEL'S RIDE TO REDEMPTION

Based on a True Story

BILLY FOURIE

REACH PUBLISHERS

Copyright © 2024 Billy Fourie

First edition 2024

All rights reserved. No part of this book may be reproduced or transmitted in any form or by any means, electronic or mechanical, including photocopying, recording or any information storage or retrieval system without permission from the copyright holder.

The Author has made every effort to trace and acknowledge sources/resources/individuals. In the event that any images/information have been incorrectly attributed or credited, the Author will be pleased to rectify these omissions at the earliest opportunity.

Published by Billy Fourie using Reach Publishers' services,
P O Box 1384, Wandsbeck, South Africa, 3631

Edited by Cara Hallier for Reach Publishers
Cover designed by Reach Publishers
Website: www.reachpublishers.org
E-mail: reach@reachpublishers.org

REACH PUBLISHERS

Billy Fourie
willrichf@gmail.com

DEDICATION

My dearest wife,

Aileen, your presence in my life from the earliest days of my journey in Christ has been a profound blessing. I am humbled by the depth of your love and care, and I thank the Lord daily for granting me such a devoted partner. As we mark 46 years together, I reflect with gratitude, knowing that not a single day has been tainted with regret. My love for you knows no bounds, extending beyond the confines of time into eternity, where we will share in His embrace.

My father,

Dad, your unwavering love, guidance, and enduring patience have sculpted the foundation of faith upon which my life stands. Your commitment to upholding Christian principles without compromise has been a beacon of light on my journey.

My mother,

Mom, words cannot express the depth of remorse for the challenges I brought upon you during your time on earth. Yet, amidst it all, your love, prayers, and unwavering faith never faltered. Your radiant smile, even in the face of adversity, and your embodiment of Christ's love in every action continue to inspire me, even on your gravestone, you asked for this verse to be inscribed:

Job 13:15: Though He slay me, yet will I trust in Him...

FOREWORD

In a world where darkness often seems to reign supreme, stories of redemption shine like beacons of hope. The true story you hold in your hands is one such beacon—a journey from the depths of despair to the heights of grace.

Through the eyes of Billy, we witness the tumultuous twists and turns of a life lived on the edge, a life marked by rebellion, addiction, and violence. Yet, woven into the fabric of this narrative is a thread of divine intervention, leading to a miraculous transformation.

As you embark on this gripping journey, prepare to be inspired, challenged, and ultimately uplifted by the power of redemption and the unyielding love of a wonderful saviour: Jesus.

TABLE OF CONTENTS

	Dedication	5
	Foreword	7
1.	Peer Pressure	11
2.	Delilah	18
3.	Getting into the Great Big World	25
4.	Render Unto Caesar	44
5.	The Fast Lane	60
6.	Further into the Gutter	78
7.	Hit the Road	86
8.	The Final 'Jol'	95
9.	The Great Deliverance	114
10.	Rise Up and Walk	127
11.	Prosper and Testing Times	140
12.	Growth and Painful Moments	147
13.	Time of Restoration	166

CHAPTER 1

PEER PRESSURE

"Please Dad, let me just go this once?" I begged.

"No! no! no! I've told you a hundred times. Don't even ask me," Dad said, with determination in his voice.

This argument was more frequent now. Regular arguments erupted in the family, even among us three brothers, who basically had the same goal: to do what we wanted. The difference was that our fights led to violence, with a knife or a chain, whatever was nearby. Where this violence is rooted,

I don't know, because my parents were so loving and full of the things of God.

We had reached a situation where we were in confrontation with our parents and school staff continuously. We began to hate them, saying they stood between us and a life of pleasure.

My friends in Grade 8 (first year of senior high school) often shared their weekend experiences. I, on the other hand, aged 12, had to make cold excuses, as my weekends were taken up by church activities which embarrassed me. I often lied about my weekends, fabricating interesting stories. Usually, my brothers and I decided what stories were to be told. I confided in a friend at school one day about my hassles with my parents. His advice to me was that I should run away from home. Today, I am reminded of the verse in the Bible that warns us: ...*Blessed is the man that walks not in the counsel of the ungodly* (Psalm 1:1).

The entire school class was vibrating with excitement as news of a well-known rock band was to 'hit' our small town the following weekend.

"This band is the best, man! Far out!" These were some of the comments coming from different young people throughout the town and schools. It was Clive, one of my schoolmates, who popped the question loudly in class one day, the question I had been dreading.

"Hey, Billy, are you coming with us Friday night to the gig?"

There was a deathly silence in the class as everyone turned to look at me to hear my answer.

"Yea man, of course. What a question, bru!"

I hastily answered, knowing full well that my parents would never allow it. But how could I tell the truth when most of these guys would just tell their parents, "Go to hell, I'll do what I like."

I tried asking my parents' permission to go, but once again they refused, explaining exactly why. Well, that was it! I had enough and made up my mind to run away from home and spend the night at Clive's house, where we would attend the gig together.

That night at the gig, I stood right up front by the stage while the band played. It was during one of the breaks that I was introduced to the band leader. I was overawed by the situation. My first live gig and I was with one of the main band members.

While listening to the band and freaking out to the rock music, Jose, a Portuguese friend from school shouted above the sound of the guitars and drums,

"Hey Bill! Make a pipe, my bru!"

At first, I had no idea what he was talking about, but threw him a thumbs up and shouted.

"Okay, let's go for it," I responded.

I had already started smoking cigarettes but was green to smoking marijuana. Jose also had very little experience, (as I found out later) because we smoked it 'neat' with no cigarette tobacco mix in the *zol* whatsoever, and smoked it still in the original thick brown paper wrapping he had bought it in.

I returned to the gig not feeling quite myself, but decided that the marijuana had had little effect on me and therefore was quite harmless. I had fallen into the trap that thousands of young people are being ensnared by today. It was the beginning of many years of addiction to 'weed' and the gateway drug to even worse.

I stayed at Clive's house that weekend. My parents had meanwhile found out where I was and, after several phone calls, sent a police squad car to collect me from Clive's house. During the journey home, I was given a long speech (and threats) about how I would eventually end up in prison or destitute on the streets.

On arriving home, my biggest fear was that my dad would beat me, which never happened. I think this hurt more than anything else. My dad, mom and sister cried and eventually I was also reduced to tears. It was a very emotional time. I knew that what I had done had hurt them very deeply, yet I felt that they and their crazy rules had robbed me of my well-deserved pleasure.

This was sadly the beginning of many more 'run aways' from home. Each time I asked permission to go out somewhere, and my parents refused, as it was going to take me down the wrong road according to them. I just packed a bag and disappeared in the night. Twice I ran away to Durban on the East Coast of South Africa and although I had no money and nowhere to stay, I would end up begging for money on the streets.

On one such occasion, Clive and I slept on the beach under the trampolines at night and by day begged for money from beachgoers. A lot of people asked questions; others ignored us completely, while others chased us away like they would stray dogs. We somehow managed to survive for quite a few days in this way and now, many years later, I realise that during those sad days, my dearest mother, father and sister would be praying earnestly for God to intervene and keep His hand of protection on me.

Many a day during these runaway *stints*, there was a deep longing for a warm bed and a nice big plate of home-cooked food, but I couldn't allow these thoughts to spoil my pleasure and I would press them into the background.

Back at school, smoking marijuana became a regular pastime. This took place behind an electrical substation at the back of the school. The marijuana was 'inserted' into a steel ballpoint pen casing, sometimes into a bottle neck, or we would just roll a 'joint'.

Sport, especially cricket, was something I enjoyed immensely and in which I achieved honours, but sadly, here too, the drug seriously affected my game. My reflexes became slower and my eye for the ball was no longer good. I began to lose interest as my game deteriorated. I also started sniffing petrol and benzene in the garage at home.

My friends became the most important thing in my life, while my family faded into the distance. My home

was just a boarding house; I came and went as I pleased. More time playing truant from school and spending time on off-road motorcycles at the top of the old gold mine slime dams.

We also visited Clive's sister a lot. She lived with a man who never worked and was heavy on drugs. They often wrote our letters to the school, excusing us for not attending and explaining our absence due to illness, etc. On one occasion, we bunked school to look after their house for two days. We had no one to write letters for us. So, I came up with a brilliant idea.

"Hey Clive, let's each break an arm," I suggested. "Then we can stay off from school a few weeks."

"Hell, that's a good idea, but how?" Clive asked.

"Try this on me," I said, reaching for a large steel

pipe lying ready nearby.

I laid my arm on the side of the windowsill and watched as Clive took careful aim, jumped up into the air, and, with all his might, brought the steel pipe swishing through the air and crashing onto my arm.

"Yeah! Yeah!" I yelled. "It's broken, dammit, it's broken!" I was now holding my left arm and running up and down the driveway shouting, "That's sore! Damn! It's sore!" After what seemed like hours, Clive calmed me down and we both looked at my arm.

"Can you move your fingers? Clive asked.

"Oh, no!" I cried. My fingers moved and there was no pain.

"Try again," I said to Clive.

"You're mad, bru," he said.

"Do it, man!" I insisted.

Well, we tried twice more, but it seemed that no bones were going to break, and we were forced to forget my 'bright' idea this time round.

CHAPTER 2

DELILAH

"Good morning, ma'am! I believe you are moving into town. Do you need help with the move?" I boldly asked our new teacher, admiring her body without shame.

"Why, thank you, Billy! That is kind of you. I will need help," she answered to my surprise.

Well, that whole Saturday was spent helping 'Miss' move and downing the dozen beers she had bought for Clive and me.

"Billy, why don't you connect the hi-fi and stay for a party?" Miss asked.

"Great idea, maybe you can get a few more drinks," I suggested.

Clive brought his girlfriend and that night we had a party. We all slept at the flat and my relationship with the teacher got more involved as time went on. Weekends were spent helping her with all kinds of home and school chores.

Before a renowned 9-hour motor car endurance race at Kyalami our national racetrack in South Africa, our drinks orders were placed with our favourite teacher and typically included three dozen beers each, two 1-litre bottles of brandy, two quarts of Cola Punch Spirits. That was for two nights and a day. The race was seldom seen.

At one such race, my friend and I met with a renowned 1% motorcycle club from Johannesburg for the first time. We made friends and they were amused that we were so young, only 13 years old and totally drunk, in our underpants, and, to top it all, we were with older women. Personally, I really liked and enjoyed what I saw: everybody at the event would take a serious detour around the gang members, avoiding contact with them at all costs. We spent the day riding around the outside of the track '3 Up' on a Triumph Bonneville motorcycle with one of the gang members and thought we were real hotshots.

Back at school, I was the talk of the staff, pupils and even friends as my relationship with the teacher became more obvious. At one stage, my mother and father paid her a visit at her apartment to find out exactly what was going on, as she was some 18 years older than me. I hated them for going to see her as they demanded that she stop seeing me. Well, not too much later, she was transferred to another school.

After an inter-school sports meeting, my brothers, some friends, and I were ordered by the vice principal of our school to pick up papers at the municipal arena after the sports function. We bluntly refused so the vice principal demanded we get into his car (about five of us) and go to the school for 'disciplinary action'.

Once again, we all refused, so the vice principal grabbed one of my school friends and forced him into the car. We immediately surrounded his car while student friends who watched the scene unfold joined us shouting, jeering, and rocking the vehicle back and forth. He shouted at us to get out of the way, but we shouted louder and louder and refused to move. Our friend inside the car was in stitches with laughter. The vice principal got out of his car and walked away, and we took our friend out of the car and ran away from the stadium.

The next day we were all called into the headmaster's office and got a whipping *Six of the Best*, as we always called it, with a heavy cane and then we had to write out 'affidavits' stating what exactly took place. My friend was expelled from the school and due to my father's pleas, my brothers and I were given a definite final warning (once again). We were also accused of assaulting the vice principal, when in fact we only gave him a ' little shove' (or two).

Things went from bad to worse at school as the conflict with the school management increased to the point where all parties were threatening to settle these constant clashes with fistfights behind closed doors.

"You, Fourie brothers, cut your hair by tomorrow or else!" It was just another normal day of threats from the school management, prefects and teachers towards me and my brothers. In hindsight, their actions were totally justifiable. We were the rebels of the school, with no respect for anyone, including the school management.

We refused to submit to the school's constant orders for haircuts. This was the hippie era; short hair was for people who had serious issues in life. The following day, because none of us had gotten haircuts, we were once again escorted into the principal's office, where he was waiting with hair clippers (can you believe it?).

I hesitantly submitted to the haircut, but my older brothers had other ideas.

"You are next, boy," the principal demanded, looking

at my brother and almost shoving me to one side.

"That will be the damned day when you cut my hair!" my brother shouted at the principal. He stood up, looked the principal straight in the eye, and marched out of the office with my other brother (his twin) hot on his trail.

I saw the shocked look on the principal's face as he stood there speechless, watching them walk out of his office.

They went back to their class, where they got their suitcases, came back into the principal's office (where I was patiently waiting), and poured the contents of their suitcases onto his desk, half eaten sandwiches and all. The result was catastrophic.

"This is what we think of you and your school, we've

had enough, you old goat!" one twin shouted.

"Don't you dare speak to me like that, you riffraff! I'll

whip you!" he shouted back at my brother.

"You and who?" the two of them yelled almost in unison, laughing, then ran out of his office with me close on their heels.

Sadly, once again, a huge headache and another problem regarding me and my brothers for my dearest father and mother to deal with.

My father tried to encourage us from an early age to attend a youth camp that was run by the church. We saw this as an opportunity to meet girls who had by now become of greater interest to us than school.

The first youth camp I attended at the age of 11 was also the first time I drank alcohol. A friend and I slipped away from camp, hitchhiked to a nearby shopping centre and bought a 'half jack' of Vodka. That night we drank the vodka and got a few girls into our tent. We were so drunk that we started to strip off our clothes and danced around the tent.

Our respect for people and the things of the Almighty God had totally gone and we were already sliding down this wide gutter, right into the mire of this world.

My whole life now revolved around friends, girls, sex, drink, and drugs. The things of God became of less and less value. The wonderful things He had done for me as a kid were now only a very vague memory. I must, however, say that deep down in my soul, there was still an enormous fear of death because I believed in heaven and hell and knew that if I died, I would be found in hell.

* * *

Due to the rapid deterioration of my schoolwork, I was forced to stay after school every afternoon for 'homework class'.

We had a 30-minute break once school had ended for the day before commencing with the homework classes. During this break, a friend and I would cycle into town and steal different items from the local stores, such as sweets, biltong and other 'tasty goodies', return to school and swap the stolen items for cigarettes, drugs and whatever was available in the class. This was also the beginning of my stealing career. I was only 14 and already involved in serious thefts, eventually escalating to mugging people for money, stealing from cars, shops, and eventually attempted armed robberies in Johannesburg and surrounding towns.

Due to my lack of interest in school and the burning desires within me for freedom, drugs, drink, and women, I told my parents I was leaving school to start work. By now, I had failed Grade 11 and was heavily into drinking and drugs. I had crumbled under the pressure (peer pressure) as well as my own inner lusts of the flesh. Not something you can see, but it's there all the time.

I had lost my backbone. The good things in life I had been taught were looking bad, and the bad things in life were looking good. I was going down with the crowds and had taken the bait of deception hook, line, and sinker.

CHAPTER 3

GETTING INTO THE GREAT BIG WORLD

"Oh no, not another day!"

Once again, I was rudely awakened by banging on the wall, accompanied by shouts and screams of "Wake up, you fool! Get out of bed! Put that music off! Shut up!"

The shouting echoed through the corridors of the three-storey apprentice hostel. All this anger was aimed at me and on top of this commotion was the sound of my vinyl hi-fi player at full pitch with my favourite rock music. My alarm was also ringing in a frenzy and my bedside lamp was shining in my face.

"Oh no!" I gasped once again. "Another day!"

I was now 16, and most evenings were spent in a drugged stupor, and it was extremely difficult to wake up in the mornings. So, to wake up, I designed a 'special alarm' to wake me up and the entire apprentice hostel where I was staying, much to their absolute hatred for me.

This is how it worked:

With the record player needle set on a selected song from a heavy rock album, the LP vinyl was set and ready to play. A light was set up from the same wall plug, with the light focused on my pillow. The wall plug switch was tied to the old type of alarm with a butterfly knob to wind it up and the clock was taped down to the desk with heavy duty tape, so as the alarm went off, the butterfly knob at the back of the alarm would wind up turning the wire I had attached to the light switch, and 'bingo' the wall switch would be turned on, thus switching on the record player, which was on full blast and at the same time switching on the bed lamp to shine into my eyes.

If the rock music and light in my eyes did not wake me, the neighbours banging on the walls and door would certainly wake me up (I hoped).

We had tried so many different methods of smoking

- marijuana, such as the traditional 'slow boat', 'bottle neck', 'clay pipe', 'hubbly bubbly', 'earth pipe' and 'bottle neck pipe'. Some days we did up to six or seven 'slow boats' and three or four 'bottle necks', and that on a weekday was nothing out of the ordinary.

Weekends were the real time to 'freak out' with a 'cheap rave' that included cough mixtures, overdoses on pain or slimming tablets, or, at times, when money was really scarce, we would even inhale benzene or petrol.

One Friday night, Jack, a fellow apprentice, suggested we break the same old routine of boozing and smoking it up and that we get out of the city and go on a 'cheap rave' and

visit a well-known hot mineral pool resort a few hours' ride out of Johannesburg.

"What will it be?" Jack asked.

"Let's go for tabs," I suggested.

"No," said Don. "Cough mixture."

So off we went looking for a day/night pharmacy and each bought a few bottles of a certain type of cough mixture. (Today you need a doctor's prescription for these very cough mixtures, as they are classified as schedule one drugs). We headed east to the resort to enjoy the weekend.

The first bottle went down with difficulty, but the second one, I do not remember much about, because suddenly, I was floating all over the place. The moon was so close, you could reach out and touch it. I was seeing all kinds of hallucinatory images. Jack was looking at the moon with his knees bent most of the weekend and would not respond to anything at all. After the weekend, it took us at least a week to try and recover from the aftereffects of the drugs.

We called this part a 'heavy downer', so one would have to either smoke more marijuana or take uppers to avoid the heavy depression attacks that come with these 'cheap raves'.

After bailing out of school at the age of 15, I started working at a telephone manufacturer, where we 'wired tele-communication racks' for automatic telephone exchange systems. The many ladies that worked at the factory loved to party, which I found out after a few weeks at work. Overtime was the time for these 'staff parties'. The factory was well-known for its drug addicts and 'hippy type' people that worked there.

"Billy! Hey, Billy!" I turned. It was Kevin, my older brother.

"You wanna come along for a bar lunch during lunch break today?" he offered.

"Great idea," I eagerly responded. Needless to say, some two hours and many beers later, we were 'totally slammed'.

"Let's go show those broads at work a thing or two," Kevin slurred.

"hell Kev, do you think we're sober enough?" I asked jokingly and headed towards the car.

On arriving at the factory, we managed to get past security and into the plant, went straight to the section where we were working and started to flirt and even fondle the girls.

One of the girls screamed, the foreman and the chargehand came running to their aid. There was an exchange of swear words, and suddenly, the place was crawling with security guards.

We were handcuffed and taken to the foreman's office, where he wrote out dismissals for both of us and the security officers escorted us out the gate with all the people in the factory looking out from the windows.

Even in my drunken state, I was embarrassed and ashamed that, at 15 years old, I couldn't even keep a steady job. I wanted to run away from those glaring eyes.

Then, I went to work at a very well-known glass factory as a furnace operator (my third job since leaving school). The hours were much longer, at times, I worked 16-hour shifts to make enough money to buy a motorcycle.

It was not long before I purchased a 1953 'Norton Dominator' 500cc motorcycle, which the owner built into a '600cc AJS frame'. The bike had a lot of chrome and wherever I went, people used to glare at this beauty. In order to purchase this motorcycle, I had to lie about my age (as I was only 15) and signed the hire purchase papers myself with a letter from my employee stating I was employed full-time, which somehow allowed me to purchase the motorcycle. Now, at last, I was in the fast lane.

My young life consisted of drink, drugs, women, and motorcycles. I thought the fun was just beginning, not knowing the brakes of my life had just failed, and I was going downhill at an incredible speed, 'pulling a tonne' (100 miles/

hour) to hell, not realising that I had fallen for this great deception at such a young age.

As soon as I turned 16, I started my apprenticeship as a fitter and turner at a military aircraft construction company. It was the 'norm' for me to smoke marijuana at work during my tea and lunch breaks. As an apprentice, I was allocated an 'artisan journeyman' who would teach me as we worked together. Our first large project was to install a 200-300-metre compressed airline outside the factory to a security gate near the South African International Airport.

The task was going to take us three to four weeks. The journeyman was also a certified alcoholic who had been to rehab many times.

So, each morning at about 9:30am, he would slip away from work and buy a 'half jack' bottle of cane spirits. He would send me to the kiosk to buy some 'mix' (lemonade), so by 1pm the 'half jack' was finished, and Dan, the journeyman, would slip away to buy a 'nip', a smaller bottle of cane.

This went on for nearly three weeks. Every day, it was the same story. I could not 'clock out' in the afternoons as I was way too drunk. When I got back to the apprentice hostel, I would get on my motorcycle and be one of the first clients at the local nightclub in Hillbrow, Johannesburg.

My body could not wait until later than 11am each day, then I would start shaking and wondering when Dan, my journeyman, would be bringing the first bottle of drink. After four weeks, I was 'relieved' in the sense that the job was nearing completion but had to smoke more marijuana to keep me on an 'upper'. The shaking got worse as my body craved the daily dose of alcohol.

One morning, I had just had enough of going to work, so I stayed off and early in the evening, I decided to break my arm so I could get off work for a few weeks. This time, it was not going to be with a lead pipe. I decided to try something I had read about vinegar, so I bought a bottle of vinegar, soaked a towel in the liquid, wrapped it around my arm, and then covered it with plastic. The next morning, I smashed my arm against the wall, shouted and screamed, but no broken arm! Damn it, these bones of mine would just not break.

* * *

The company sent me to a technical college for three months to study further. Each morning was spent waiting at the station for a girl I knew who worked in Johannesburg. She would get off the train, have a chat and then I would catch the next train with her to Johannesburg, where we would 'smoke it up' and go to the movies or spend the day in a hotel room instead of going to work and college.

At one stage, she told me that she was having difficulty making excuses as to why she was not at work. I didn't care, as long as we could 'freak out' for a few hours.

Since my school days, I had had a tremendous problem controlling my sex drive. Most young men and women can either control the tremendous urge by channelling it into sports activities, etc., or they can abuse it. I chose the latter, to my disgrace and regret. It was believed by most drug users that you haven't had sex unless you have it all drugged-up. Well, I must tell you, it's another lie from the Devil.

Sex can only be enjoyed to its fullest if it takes place under the umbrella of marriage and each partner is completely sober.

The lack of control over my sexual desires led me into very, very serious problems at least three times in my life. I could never even write about that because of the seriousness of the problems and the innocent women involved, not to mention the consequences for all, but I pray that God will give them grace, strength and comfort as they live with the consequences, and I live with the regret. I thank the Lord for His great, forgiving power and restoration.

My language deteriorated, and I only spoke 'slang' and could not conduct a decent conversation with normal people. I became very withdrawn. Marijuana gave me a kind of complex where I only felt secure and confident when I was with other drug users, or so-called friends. The urge and uncontrollable desire to steal also got worse every time I had alcohol mixed with drugs.

One night, at a disco with a good friend, I was very drunk and drugged-up and went outside to do the usual, which was to break into cars and look for 'goodies'. Having tried some five or six cars that were either empty or too difficult to open, I noticed through the window of a vehicle what looked like a flat suitcase sticking out from under the driver's seat. I knew immediately that I was on to something good!

So, with my piece of wire, I managed to get into the car, sat in the driver's seat, checked around to see if all was safe, closed the door and opened the suitcase. Wow! Jackpot! Rings—at least fifty of them, each in its own little slot and it looked as if some had diamonds. I stuffed my pockets full, checked the rest of the car and decided to open the boot.

Bingo! Another suitcase full of necklaces. Those I stuffed inside my shirt. I closed the vehicle up again and ran with excitement to tell Jack of my findings. I found him on the dance floor with a young girl.

"Hey Jack! Look what I got," I said eagerly, opening the front of my shirt. Jack took one look and started cursing me.

"Get away from me, you Devil. I hate you, bru! You've got a serious problem—sort it out!" Jack shouted at the top of his voice.

For the first time in my life, I was worried about my condition and wondered if there was any hope for me, because now even my friends, who were just as bad, were beginning to hate the things I was doing. This hatred was causing me to feel deeply rejected, lonely and lost, yet I would not turn to God. I began turning this hopelessness into a definite hatred for everyone. Was there someone who could help me? I could hear my dad's words in my ears.

"My boy, Jesus will never give up on you. He will be waiting. Don't be too proud to turn to Him."

There were times I even longed for our family outings, reminiscing about just how innocent I was then, when life had seemed so clean. Mom and Dad were so happy and indeed, all of us were happy. What had gone wrong? How did I end up this way? These thoughts and questions ran through my mind repeatedly.

As I ran outside, away from the disco and Jack, with a tremendous feeling of rejection, I took out the jewellery I had just stolen and threw it as far as I could into an open field. In this terrible state of depression and rejection, I walked home hating myself for what I had become.

Saturdays were spent going from one bar to another, with the first drinks being ordered at 10am. We played darts or pool and by 5pm, we would look for something to eat, have a few more beers, then head off to a 'session' (live rock band) or disco to find some action. On our way there, we would smoke a few marijuana pipes laced with mandrax to stabilise us slightly, but that usually put us in another lethargic world and our aggression seemed to have vanished.

Sundays were spent in the country smoking marijuana so that we could 'enjoy' nature. Now I know that nature can only be enjoyed fully when you know the Creator. My life was monotonous—it became a mere existence; I was looking for stronger drugs and way more action and could somehow never find satisfaction.

We tried all kinds of things to break the monotony of being drugged-up with the same old things; some of these were inhaling benzene, eating 'malpitte' (seeds from a wild plant) or even sniffing glue and eating the inside of certain 'nose inhalers,' but it always came back to the old routine. We spoke a lot about 'shooting the needle' or 'spiking' (that is mainline), but we were a little wary, and just as well,

Praise God, as that would have been the beginning of the end with no turning back like 'pulling a tonne to death'.

On this one occasion, Jack, Deon, Don and I went in a 'souped up' (full house high speed engine) car to a pleasure resort in the eastern part of the country, near to Kruger National Park. The car was rebored maximum with a high lifting cam—'the works.'

With music blaring at full volume, the inside of the car filled with marijuana smoke and beers being passed around, I shouted, "Here's another one; step on it, Jack! Give this baby a go!"

Every car on the road was a likely 'dice'. None of them could stay with us over the 160km/h range. All the way to the resort, we were drinking beers and smoking marijuana. I must say, we must have looked quite a sight with shoulder-length hair, beards, red eyes, stinking of alcohol, leather jackets and denim jeans. Two days later, we were chased away from the resort because of our drunken misbehaviour. On the way home, the 'souped up' Ford Anglia we were travelling in 'blew the engine'.

Jack and Deon hitchhiked to the nearest small town, i.e. Witbank, to fetch a tow truck, while Don and I were left with an 'arm of marijuana', as we used to call it, which was a roll of marijuana the length and thickness of a large man's arm. With no food and no water at our disposal, we decided to start smoking the arm of marijuana that was left over. This was at about 10am in the morning and we finished the entire 'arm' of marijuana by 5pm and must have passed out because we were rudely awoken by laughing and shouting. It was Jack and Deon.

"Hey, wake up! Make a pipe!" Jack shouted.

"Sorry, bru, you are too late! It's all finished," Don laughingly answered.

"Damn it!" Deon exclaimed. "I need something to calm me down."

"We got into a scrap with some guys at a hotel and one of the bastards knifed Deon," Jack said. "We had to get him stitched up at the hospital first before coming here."

"Okay, let's go get them," Don and I suggested, eager for a fight.

"Okay," Jack said. "Let's just get this damn car out of here."

So, because we had no tow truck when the engine blew on the Anglia, Jack left Deon in the bar on their way earlier and got a lift to his house some two hours away, managed to collect his own souped-up vehicle, which was an old V8 Studebaker Lark. He returned to the hotel to collect Deon, who had been in a fight and cut up. Now we had to tow the vehicle ourselves with two 'mother drunk' and two totally 'goofed out' dudes, one with a stitched-up arm. This spelled total disaster, which in fact was coming.

Don and I decided we would split ourselves up just to balance out the odds—better one drunken person and one drugged person in a vehicle than two in the same state we reckoned. Jack and Don were in the V8 Studebaker

Lark and I could ride with Deon in the car with the blown engine, the one being towed. Deon took the wheel.

About 10km outside a little town called Carolina, while we were being towed (according to Don later) at about 140km per hour, my driver, Deon, passed out from all the drugs and alcohol he had consumed as well as the pain tablets the hospital gave him.

The vehicle left the road at a right angle and must have rolled a few times. It seemed as if everything was happening in slow motion. I remember rolling inside the car—we didn't wear safety belts—I could feel gravel falling down the back of my neck and my body being thrown from side to side as we went through the rolls. It felt like it was never going to stop, then suddenly, it was all over, and a deathly silence followed. It was very dark. I immediately felt that I was still in one piece and how strange that I was now totally sober.

Looking around, I could see very little except that the roof of the car was squashed in and the front windscreen was gone, but the space was a possible way for me to get out as the doors were both crushed. Deon was missing. I managed to creep out of the front area where the windscreen used to be, looking around and listening for any sign of life or at least the vehicle that had been towing us, but there was nothing and with Deon missing, I backtracked in the direction I suspected we had left the main road.

That was when I heard the sound of someone shouting way off in the bushes. It was about 80-100 metres from the car. It was Deon; his knife wound had opened again, there was blood all over and he kept shouting that he was cold. All I could find was a sheet that had fallen out of my suitcase. I covered him with the white sheet and to crown it all, it was now about 2:30am and a thick mist had set over the area and a slight drizzle. Jack and Don, who were towing us, did not even know we were no longer on tow until they arrived in the next town, i.e. Carolina, which was some 10km from where we parted ways.

We heard from them later, that on arrival at the town, they decided to stop at the garage and check on us, only to find that the rope had snapped and Deon, Billy and the car were nowhere to be found.

Don said himself and Jack had a discussion to try and determine at what point the rope had broken. They made the decision to drive back slowly hooting and shouting as they went. I heard what sounded like a hooter in the distance: bah! bah! bah! bah! Following the sound, I ran in its direction and towards the main road approximately 500 metres through the maize fields towards the main road. When they found me, they asked where the car was, I explained it was some 500 metres in the maize field. On arrival at the vehicle, they both saw the body with a white sheet covering it totally.

Jack jumped out of the car, screaming and crying.

"Deon, I'm sorry! I'm sorry, my bru. I did not want you to die, bru! Oh God, forgive me; I did not want him to die. Oh God, please forgive me!"

He kept shouting so I started laughing and said, "He's only cold, you idiot, not dead."

Jack was furious with me, but Deon started to laugh as well and that made us all laugh.

Not really something to laugh about.

As the mist cleared and it got lighter, we saw that the car had knocked over a milestone, broken a telephone pole in half (that was when Deon was thrown out), flipped over a barbed wire fence without touching it and landed in the maize field on its roof 500 metres from the main road.

Looking at the wrecked car, I realised this was too close, and that if I had been killed in that accident, I would have gone straight to hell. There had been no chance to quickly ask forgiveness, as I used to think I would. It had all happened way too fast. This was the first of two very close encounters with death.

God had not given up on me yet. I still had a family that was praying for my salvation and for my return to the throne of grace.

The verse in the Bible came to mind: *You fool this night, your soul shall be required of you* (Luke 12:19-21).

I wondered whether this was God talking to me. Man, if only I would give Him a chance! While I was deep in thought, my mate's voice rang in my ears.

"Hey Billy, you sure got out of this one bru. How do you do it, my bru?" Jack asked.

"Must be luck," I replied with a fake laugh.

Everyone burst out laughing. Someone piped up, "The Devil looks after his own. Ha! Ha! Ha!"

I laughed; this is what mattered most—me and my mates. But somewhere in the back of my mind, a fear gripped my heart. I knew that if I had died in that car, I would certainly not have been ready to step into eternity. The Bible says: *It is appointed unto man once to die, after that the judgement* (Hebrews 9:27).

The time was drawing near for me to do my compulsory military training. I was seconded to the South African Navy in Simonstown, and in a way, I was looking forward to my training, as I also needed a change from this monotonous existence of drugs, alcohol and friends.

Don, Jack, Deon, and I decided that we all deserve a good holiday, especially me, seeing I was going to the navy. The venue was to be Durban on the east coast of South Africa, and we would stay in the city centre as this would give us easy access to hard-core (opium) drug suppliers.

On arriving in Durban, on the east coast of South Africa, our first visit was to the old market, where we were offered everything from prostitutes to pistols. We placed our order for 'opium', 'Durban poison' (quality marijuana), mandrax to smoke in our marijuana pipe and a *'jalompie'* (clay) pipe for each of us.

While we waited for the order, we were invited to 'make a pipe' with the merchants in a private car park (basically to make sure we were not undercover narcs). A constant eye was kept for the 'fuzz' (police) and only after we had 'bust a pipe' did they have confidence that we were not narcs, but the real deal.

"Hey, you brus are okay," one of the merchants said, smiling. A signal was given to someone across the car park and suddenly it was there, the 'works'. The full order and an exchange of money took place and off we went. The next few days were spent in the hotel room smoking opium laced with mandrax and our high-quality 'Durban Poison'.

It was now Old Year's Eve, and Clive and I sat at a well-known hotel on the beachfront consuming a few beers. People were starting to gather for the Old Year's Eve festivities.

"Hey Don, let's go back to the hotel for some of the good stuff (opium)," I suggested.

We ran back to the hotel in a drunken and drugged-up state, ordered a few beers each from room service, cut our share of the opium into little squares and started eating it. We were so drugged and drunk that we decided to eat the opium and not smoke it while washing it down with the beers. We knew you were supposed to smoke the stuff, but we wanted to eat it for some totally unknown, obscure reason.

The result was disastrous. We were running all over town, not knowing what was going on because all the cars were hooting like crazy, and we thought they were hooting at us, but it was, in fact, Old Year's Eve. I felt like I was losing my mind. We came around two days later in the hotel room, only to continue with our alcohol and drug binge.

After we had ordered beers on one of the days, the waiter who brought the drinks kept sniffing as he put them down on our entrance table. He walked out of the room, and we suspected trouble. About five minutes later, there was a knock at the door and a man who called himself the hotel detective, together with the manager, and security ordered us to leave the hotel immediately. This was a tragedy for us at that point, as half the opium and marijuana were still taped to the back of the dressing table drawer and with these dudes standing over us as we packed our few belongings, we had to leave all our 'stash' where it was.

We decided to move further south to the small but popular beach town of Margate, where we spent another week binging on alcohol and drugs.

When I returned home, my parents commented that I was very pale, with large black rings around my eyes and did not look as if I had taken a holiday before I was to be shipped off to the South African Navy in Simonstown.

Well, if this was getting into the Great Big World, somehow it was not what I had expected. The 'Great Big World' (my world) was really very small, with only a handful of drug addicts and dropouts as friends and by the look of things, my life was in fact a mess and certainly not as full of pleasure and happiness as was expected.

1971 The last photo of me (long hair) with my dearest mom, beside her is Dad, eldest brother and two youngest siblings. I was 16 years old.

CHAPTER 4

RENDER UNTO CAESAR

In the train compartment, there was deadly silence, only the noise of the train wheels on the track could be heard as it rattled off a monotonous rhythm. My mind went back to the scene we had just left behind at Johannesburg Station. Thousands of weeping mothers, sisters, and girlfriends. Proud fathers stood quietly, looking on as their sons left for their compulsory military service in the South African Navy.

For me, it was a means of escaping the mess my life was in. I really wanted to see if I could be 'normal' again and somehow shake this drug habit I was caught in. The silence in the compartment was broken as the door slid open and a uniformed man peered in and shouted:

"Attention!" I looked at this dude and thought, *Okay, what now?*

"Stand up roof!" Literally meaning, 'scab'.

"Civvy (civilian) street is now gone!"

"You!" he shouted pointing at me. "Cut your beard or no food till we get to Cape Town!" Which would have been some 12 hours later.

Well, the shouting continued for the next few weeks, but something worse was waiting for me—withdrawal. I would wake up in the middle of the night with the sheets sopping wet and my body shaking and in a sweat. This continued for about two weeks, but the busy routine somehow helped to keep my mind off drugs and drink.

We were given a list of all the areas in Cape Town that were out of bounds for South African sailors. So, our first weekend pass was spent exploring every nightclub and red-light area (on the 'out of bounds' list) in Cape Town.

I once again started drinking heavily but laid off the drugs until I could get a trustworthy supplier, so each weekend when we received a 'weekend pass' was spent in one of Cape Town's many nightclubs.

After my basic training, I was transferred to an inland base in Goodwood to specialise as an engine room mechanic for the ships. Now only 17 years old, it was awesome to know that I was going to experience life on the only destroyer the South African Military owned, i.e. JVR (Jan Van Riebeeck).

One day, I was called into the captain's office and asked if I would like to go home for the Easter weekend. There was one seat available on the military aircraft, and I had been chosen because I had achieved the best results during the engine room mechanic course. Many years later, I realised that it was really an answer to somebody's prayer, as this was the last opportunity I had to see my mother in good health.

As usual, the minute I got home, I contacted my friends to fetch me so we could get into some serious drinking and drug-taking. During that Easter weekend, I hardly saw my family and then it was time to return to camp. A weekend wasted with drugs, friends and very little family connection.

On my return to the naval military base, I met Peter, a professional surfer from East London who was in the same division as I was. We smoked marijuana every morning before the morning parade and every afternoon after 'knock-off time'. It was here that things started going horribly wrong again.

A lot of our time was spent in the Goodwood and Parow hotels drinking, playing darts, and smoking marijuana.

We met some girls in the hotel who stayed in the suburbs of Bellville and started visiting them on regular occasions with only the wrong intentions.

One night, one of the girls stole a bottle of her dad's 15-year-old brandy, which Peter and I finished 'neat' (without any mix). That night we destroyed shrubs in people's gardens. I jumped off a moving bus and broke the peak of my navy cap as well as tearing my 'step out' naval suit. I also threw a rock through a massive window of a very popular five-star hotel in Goodwood.

Two days later, my friend and I were called into the base captain's office. I was told I had 24 hours to get the money to pay for the window and I was given extra duties and confined to barracks for two weeks. Those two weeks were spent in a permanent, drugged-up state as sailor friends brought me whatever I needed.

I took ill after being forced to run a naval marathon in my very unfit and drugged-up state. This resulted in my being rushed to a military hospital and spending a few weeks there. The doctors soon realised that I was a drug addict and moved me to the psychiatric ward to 'dry me out'. Most of the patients in this ward were either alcoholics who were having the 'DTs' or drug addicts like myself.

It was during this time that the destroyer warship I had been seconded to left for sea, and I was sent back to a land base.

It wasn't a week, and I was back 'on the wagon' smoking marijuana and lacing it with hard drugs. We also started 'popping pills' like LSD. Meanwhile, the time for my seven-day pass was drawing nearer.

My 'seven-day pass' (the only long leave you get for one-year compulsory service) arrived and it was time to go home. We had train tickets from Cape Town to Johannesburg.

At the station, I decided to phone my parents from a phone booth and tell them I was coming home. My uncle answered the phone. I couldn't understand why, on earth, he would answer the phone at my house. He gave me the bad news: my mother was very ill. He said he would tell her and my father that I was coming home on a pass.

On arriving home, I opened the front door, and something struck me like a bomb: the house had lost its radiancy. The smell of good home cooking was replaced by an awful smell of death.

"Hello, my boy," were my father's words. He was happy to see me, yet in his eyes, I could see gloom and despair.

We spoke for a while, and I asked, "Where's Mom?" Dad answered, "Your mother is very sick, my boy; she's... busy... dying."

"No," I cried to myself. "No, God! Don't do this to us, we need our mother."

I walked into the room where she lay, very pale, with black rings around her eyes, yet she was smiling.

"Hello, my boy. How are you?" We embraced, and I wept and clung to her, hoping that everyone was wrong—Dad, the doctors, everyone—she must live.

I had a tattoo done on my arm whilst in the navy and was hoping my mom would not see it; however, it was the very first thing she noticed and pointed to my arm.

"Wow! My boy, you are no longer my little boy, but you have become a man. How lovely is that eagle. Very nice my boy!"

She looked me straight in the eye and I knew she meant it and was not being sarcastic. I hated myself for many years for doing that to my dearest mother. For most of my life since that day, I have tried to hide my tattoo from friends, family and work colleagues, not for any other reason but for my dearest mother.

With all this going on in my head, one would imagine that I would stay at her bedside, embrace her, help her, and talk to her, but instead I couldn't wait to phone my mates and ask them to fetch me, as I only had a seven-day pass. Each day, they would be there to pick me up and we would drink, smoke marijuana and just 'freak out'.

During the day, I would go to town and play pool. I never spent more than ten minutes at my dying mother's side. Today, so many years later, I still weep and think to myself if only I had been a better son, one that she could have been proud of... Instead, I was a shame to my wonderful family, especially my dearest mother, father, and sister.

It was about the fifth day that I was home that my mother got worse. The doctor was called, and he told my father that my mother's time was now very close. My father phoned the pastor, family, and friends in their church. Later that afternoon, they arrived and started to sing hymns; they were in her room, the kitchen, the lounge, the dining room, some even standing outside.

However, I was not going to sit around and sing hymns! No, sir, I only had a seven-day pass (how selfish and evil... Sic bru!).

I remember giving my mother a kiss, or rather, a peck on the cheek and off I went, not realising I was never ever going to see her again on this earth (what an absolute fool I was!). She had done nothing in her life but show me and my brothers absolute love and care, and most importantly, taught us about the love of Jesus, who was her Lord and Saviour. I really loved her so much, yet somehow the *deceitfulness* of this current world, the lust of the flesh and the short-lived pleasures of life and friends had come between me and her, not to mention between me and a loving God.

Today, I hold onto the great hope that I will see her in the mansions of glory one day. How I long to see her face-to-face and allow her to be proud of me, of what I became and not who I was when she left us.

That night I spent with my friends, making what we would call in the drug world a 'hot box'. That is when all the air vents, windows, and any place where smoke can escape the vehicle are sealed. We smoked one marijuana pipe laced with hard-core drugs after another and the smoke filled the vehicle—a thick, dense smoke that in turn, we inhaled again and again.

The heavy beat of the music caused the vehicle to shake gradually from side to side. We were in a world of our own.

The 'hot box' had cast all four of us into a deep, drugged trance. The alley we were parked in was dark, dismal, cold, and somehow added a Devilish touch to the beat of Iron Butterfly's music.

Jack was the first one to sit up as a ray of light beamed onto the vehicle, causing life and movement in the dark alley as rats scurried off to find shelter.

I shouted, "Start the damn car; let's split. It's the fuzz (cops)!"

We were racing away from the cops and, at the same time, throwing away packets of marijuana, pipes, drugs, and a flick knife I had gotten from Mozambique. We could hear a siren getting closer and with flashing lights, it wasn't long before we were pulled off the road.

"Get out, you rubbish!"

The doors were flung open, and at least four plain-clothes policemen (the drug squad) stood waiting. With music still echoing, we submitted sullenly to the physical search as well as the searching of the vehicle.

"Hey guys!" shouted the one policeman to the others.

"This car stinks of marijuana, let's take them in."

"Keep looking," was the reply.

"We need proof to lock these druggies up for a long time."

I knew we still had about 2kgs of marijuana stashed in a secret place in the boot and hoped the cops wouldn't take us in or call for the dog unit to sniff the vehicle out. They searched the car from front to back, over and over, but found nothing.

"Take their names and addresses!" the cop in charge shouted.

"You lucky bastards, I'll be watching you day and night and when I catch you, I'll put you away for a long time."

We decided to stop off at the local roadhouse to get a drink, as our mouths were dry and we needed to compose ourselves again.

While we were sitting in the car discussing our near 'bust', there was a knock at the window on my side of the car, it was my cousin.

I opened to say hi and all he said was, "Billy, I think you better go home; your mother passed away half an hour ago."

I was so drugged up that I didn't know what to say or do.

Jack said, "Billy, you must go home."

All the way home, my biggest concern was that I couldn't cry. I felt no emotion at all. I tried everything, thinking of sad things—but nothing.

When they dropped me at my house, the 'morgue van' was standing in the driveway and all the people from the church were standing on the veranda. I knew they would see that I was drugged up, so I ran down the road, rubbing my eyes and putting spit (the little I had, because marijuana and drugs dry your mouth out) on my eyes so that my dad and the church people would think that I was crying. I walked back home, ran into my old bedroom, lay down on the bed, hoping no one would follow me. Luckily, no one did.

I was given permission by the South African Navy to stay two extra days for my mother's funeral. The tragedy remained that I lost my precious mother at the age of 17 whilst I was doing compulsory military service.

My twin brothers in front of me (I'm in navy uniform) and my three uncles carrying my dearest mother's coffin, my father cradles my youngest brother in his arms and my sister behind him in a white dress with my younger sister holding her hand.

It was only when returning to Cape Town on the train that I cried and cried. Today, I still weep over all those wasted years when I had ample opportunity to show love and affection towards my mother and those who really cared for me but did not, because I was way too consumed by self-gratification.

Back at naval base, the ship I was seconded to had left port and was making its way north along the west coast. So, I was placed in an office to assist with military paperwork. This gave me more time after work to spend drinking, smoking marijuana, and moving from nightclub to nightclub in Cape Town.

One night, after supper, I was walking back to the dormitory when I heard someone shout my name.

"Billy. Hey, Billy!"

I stopped. It was a young Cape Malay sailor off one of our naval vessels.

"My name's Wally." He reached out his hand.

"Howzit," I grabbed his hand with a firm handshake.

"I believe you make a pipe," (marijuana pipe) he asked warily.

Looking into his eyes, I knew he did too and answered, "So what?"

"Come and bust a 'manny pipe' (marijuana pipe laced with mandrax methaqualone tablets) with us," Wally invited.

So off I went to bust another 'white pipe', as it is also known.

This wasn't the first time I had smoked marijuana laced with different drugs. We made about a dozen pipes, and somewhere in between, I 'freaked out'. I found myself in a disco with music pounding in my head and what looked like humans floating around a dance floor.

Two nights later, Wally invited me to 'split a cap of acid' with him and two of his cousins. This 'acid', also known as LSD, was known as 'California sunshine' and it was said to enter South Africa only once a year. The 'cap' is only as big as a pin head.

We rode to the beach and Wally mixed the 'cap of acid' in water and carefully poured each one of his shares of the LSD into polystyrene cups.

"Cheers," Wally said, holding his cup high in the air.

"Cheers," came the answer from the three of us, almost in harmony, before swallowing the LSD.

Immediately after taking the drug, we made a marijuana joint, sat back in Wally's car and waited, the music pounding away in the car. I remember nothing else.

It was about a week later that I woke up shaking in bed. I was hungry and needed to find out what was going on. When I heard that a week had passed and that I had attended morning parades with a dull look on my face, I was just about destroyed.

"Billy!" came a shout. It was Wally. "How's the trip?" he asked.

"Cool man, cool," I answered, but I didn't really enjoy it.

The local guys from the cape flats showed me how to smoke marijuana through a brick, tin, or orange and even how to make a wine/marijuana 'hubbly bubbly' and drink the wine afterwards. Each time we explored new ways of getting our fix and finding ourselves in a bombed-out state of mind and body.

On one of my weekend passes, I was invited to a 21st birthday party at Hermanus Bay. The first night of the weekend was spent in a local hotel drinking. It only took a couple of drinks, and I went outside to start stealing from cars. This time, I found quite a lot of cash and bought drinks for my friends. The next day we 'passed out' on the beach after finishing two 4.5 litre bottles of wine and the night of the 21st was spent dancing and drinking myself into a stupor.

The rest of my military training was spent trying every available drug and looking for some kind of joy and fulfilment.

One of the drivers at camp lived on a large wine farm with his parents. Each Sunday night, he brought boxes of wine to camp, which my friend and I finished in short order.

There were regular invitations to different homes over the weekends. One of these was a trip to the holiday home of a well-known Springbok surfer who occasionally smoked marijuana with us.

I began to get tired of the same old smoking marijuana being 'goofed', drinking alcohol, etc., and I desperately needed a change. Wake up, make a pipe, then off to the parade ground for the roll call, then at least 8-12 joints and pipes before 4pm This was the same old daily routine. After 4pm, it was more drugs, drinks and nightclubs. There was no more 'acid' available, so I started on nose inhalers. The inside of the inhaler was eaten (only a certain type that is not available any more).

One night, I was excited about getting high on inhalers and going to a club in town. My chemist was still open.

"Good evening, could I have one… eh… nose inhaler?" I asked the young chemist attendant.

She gave me a dirty look, said she was coming now and went to the back of the pharmacy. Suddenly, a man in a white hospital-type uniform appeared.

"Get out of here, you scum!" he blurted out in front of everyone.

"I've been watching you for weeks. The military police know all about you," he added.

I turned and ran out of the shop and down the street, scared, but knowing I must have the stuff or suffer. I caught the next bus to the small town of Bellville and tried one of my other regular chemists.

"What do you want it for?" the chemist asked suspiciously.

"My friend's got a bad cold," I answered.

"But I've seen you before. You buy these inhalers almost every second day. Give me your name and force number," he suggested.

"Forget it," I said and walked out.

I was becoming super desperate. Inside, I was shouting, "Somebody help me! I need this inhaler and will do anything to get it, even kill if I have to."

My body was now shaking from desperation. The day was not yet over, so I took a bus ride into the city (Cape Town) to try and find an emergency chemist. The journey by bus seemed to last forever. When the bus finally stopped, I jumped off, ran to the day/night chemist and finally got the nose inhaler.

My insides were consumed together with at least three or four beers, and yes, the next day came the 'heavy downer', which made me feel like I wanted to die. Well, I had learned by now that a few pep pills (uppers) and a few joints was the only way to get myself back on track to look fairly normal again until next time. What a state I was in! Oh God! Who can save me from myself?

Weekends were spent in a subculture of drugs, sex and excessive drinking, yet there always seemed to be an emptiness, a vacuum that never seemed to be filled. There were days when my thoughts would go back to my mom, dad, my brothers, and sister and how at times we would play church at home. I had no doubt in my heart that my entire family loved Jesus, but these thoughts were soon replaced by evil desires. Without fail, each night there was an incredible urge to do so (in hindsight) to satisfy my ever-growing evil desires, yet it was never really satisfied.

The 19th of December arrived, and it was time to leave the navy I had turned 18 while doing my compulsory service. The excitement was not as great as I had expected. I dragged my *balsak* (large canvas tog bag) nearer as it was too heavy to carry; my complete naval kit was inside.

I sat down, propping myself up against it and looked into the sky. I remember thinking to myself that this was now the last day of our compulsory military training. With the sun beating down and the normal old military story 'hurry up and wait', with a buzz of excitement in the air around me, everybody was glad that we're finally going home. Groups had gathered, some laughing, others bragging about what they were going to do on their arrival back home.

However, as this buzz was around me, I realised I was not at all as excited as the rest of the troops, because home meant nothing to me, work even less and 'civvy street' (civilian) was right at the bottom of the hat. All that lay ahead for me was a very dark and gloomy tunnel with not even the slightest ray of light on the other side to look forward to. In fact, it was then that I knew without a doubt that I was sinking once again into deep depression, exactly the opposite of how the rest of the troops were feeling.

I had somehow become a slave, with chains around my feet, hands and entire body. They were heavy and cold. It was then that I got up and looked down at my body, expecting to see these heavy cold chains, but, can you believe it? There was absolutely nothing! They had felt so real, but I couldn't see them; I thought I was going through drug paranoia. If only somebody could understand what I was going through, I desperately needed help. Oh, God! Is there any hope for me?

CHAPTER 5

THE FAST LANE

Well, back home, things hadn't changed much, except that the loving, kind, and shining face of my mother was now missing. The house seemed so empty and quiet. I felt so sorry for my younger brother and sister, yet I didn't do much to comfort them and make their lives a little more joyous and happier. Instead, there was only one life that mattered to me and that was mine.

It did not take long, and I was back on the drug scene with my old buddies. A new type of acid (LSD) had just hit the market and it was known as 'strawberry fields'. A lot of young people were into this scene, and I was now 18, so I joined the band wagon. I decided to leave home and move back to the hostel. I also realised that I was in serious trouble regarding drugs and my evil desires. I found it more difficult to hide the fact that I was on drugs. I was becoming like an animal.

Every time I was on drugs, evil desires and lusts would take over my life, and I seemed to have absolutely no control over anything. I felt like I had lost control. I moved into the single quarters of the company where I was working. Unfortunately, the 'social club' was only some 300 metres from the hostel, so my evenings were spent drinking and smoking dagga, until I was barred from the club for drunkenness and fighting. Every day, I could not wait for the siren to go off at 4pm which meant it was 'knock off time'. How I lived for that moment! Now I could grab a shower, get dressed and 'shoot' through to Hillbrow (or the Bronx, as we used to call it) in Johannesburg. By this time, I knew most of the regulars in the nightclubs.

"Hi Billy!" It was the barmaid in the club. "It's going to be a long, heavy evening," she shouted as the music thumped in the background.

"What will you be drinking tonight, Billy, the usual?" "Absolutely give a man a No. 17 with a little bit of love," (which is what we used to call Lion Lager beer. So, if you turn the bottle of beer upside down, LION becomes NO17) I shouted above the music. As I poured the beer, I sat back and scanned the club. It wasn't full yet, but it would be shortly. Then the party would begin, and it would go on until the early hours of the morning.

There was no great excitement at the thought of living it up again; this had become my daily routine. One thing that did grip me, however, was the journey back to the hostel at about 01:30am, because I would ride around the city and break into cars, hoping to find some valuables that I could sell to pawn shops for money, for drinks and drugs.

Some three to four months after I had completed my military training, I was paid out a small lump sum of money by my employers, which I used to buy a small convertible sports car (Triumph Spitfire Mark 3).

I found myself in the 'fast lane' with a fast sports car, fast women, booze and drugs. Every night, Monday to Sunday, was spent in the nightclub. I would often sneak half a dozen beers out of the club. My car was parked in one of the upstairs garages. I would pay the cashier the amount due at the bottom and warn him to open the boom. With the beers between my legs, I would race down to ground level at a fanatical speed and out onto the main road. The trip back to the hostel was done in record time. I seldom knew how I got home at night. After the nightclub I would find a quiet spot where I would smoke marijuana and 'freak out' until two to three in the morning. The average amount of sleep I enjoyed in 24 hours was probably around three hours in bed and about two hours at work on the toilet.

One afternoon, after work, I was returning from 'making a marijuana pipe', when the hair on my neck rose to the thundering sound of a bike engine being pushed to maximum 'revs'. She (the bike) had what sounded like 'straight throughs'. It had been a long time since I had heard a bike with megaphones and no baffles. My heart began beating faster, my steps started stretching and I broke into a slight jog. The guy on the bike was wanting everything the bike could offer as he came flying past me. The ground itself was vibrating from the power of the 750cc 4-cylinder engine.

"Howzit!" I shouted at the top of my voice as he shot past, hoping he would hear. There were brake lights, a gearing down as he reigned in the horses, bringing the beautiful steel beast to a screeching standstill. I was beginning to shake with excitement. He threw a doughnut (360° turn) and pulled up beside me.

"Howzit, bru, the name's Nic." He stretched out his hand.

I took it, squeezed it hard and said, "Billy. Good meeting ya. She's got a slight miss, but a beautiful bike, bru." I suggested pointing to the 750cc Honda 4-cylinder.

"Think you can set her?" Nic asked. We fiddled around with the carburettors for a while until she was purring like a lioness.

"Want to take her for a spin?" Nic asked.

"hell, you bet!" I eagerly replied.

Getting back on a bike did something inside of me. I loved pushing her up to 'full taps' in each gear. As we took the long straight to Bonaero Park, I felt a hard whack on the left side of my face. I was dazed for a few seconds and started to gear down and brake, not knowing what had happened, only to find out that a large bird had flown into the side of my face, killing itself and splattering its 'guts' all over me. I was a little hesitant to ride further, but nevertheless, I slowly rode back to the hostel, thinking about what had happened and how easily it could have been both of us, instead of just the bird.

One Sunday morning, I was invited by Nic and a group of his friends to spend the day at Zoo Lake. We stopped at Cafe Shebeen in Johannesburg, where we bought a few bottles of drinks. We ended up terrorising people at the Lake and overturning the boats.

Around six o'clock, Nic said, "Hey Billy, me and my mates are going to a meeting."

Jokingly, I questioned if it was a church meeting, being a Sunday, but he laughed and told me that it was a well-known motorcycle crew that meets in a boxing club. I immediately wanted to know more, telling him that I had known some of the members of the crew from my school days.

From that day on, I wanted to sell my car and buy a bike again. Nick and I became more friendly. We spent a day on 'Joule Street' going from one second-hand car dealer to the next looking for a good price for my car. Finally, we got a good deal on my car and walked out with a cheque. I had already found out about a BMW R60/US motorcycle that was going for a good price at a well-known motorcycle dealer. The deposit was paid, and a day later, the bike was mine. It had happened; I had fallen in love. There was a short marriage ceremony with this beautiful black monster, which involved all kinds of perverse sexual acts, smoking marijuana and, of course, boozing it up.

I desperately needed time off work to get used to my new wife (bike). I heard about a doctor in Boksburg who was very sympathetic towards the younger generation, especially the members of the motorcycle club. He would book me off sick for a day, week, or whatever I needed. I remember getting a large amount of marijuana and just riding all over the country. A lot of time was spent cleaning and riding this beautiful beast.

Nic came over to my room one afternoon after work. "Hey, Bill! I've organised for you to meet one of the older 'crew members' at his place tonight."

I was very glad and excited. We went to this guy's flat and spent time looking through his many photo albums of the crew. What I saw awoke the desire I had had for many years, and I asked how I could join. I was told that I would have to get to know a few more members and get into the crowd, without getting into the crowd (which doesn't make much sense, but I was determined to try). I went to a lot of 'heavy' parties, sessions, etc., and so I got to know a lot of them.

Then, one night, I went up to the leader and asked him if I could ride with 'the crew'. The co-leader came and looked at my 'wife' and seemed to like her as we were both BMW fans. I was told to 'tag along'.

My life took on a whole new meaning. I wanted everybody to know that I was part of a crew, and I was proud of what

I was. If anyone dared to speak badly of them, I wouldn't hesitate to sort them out. I had to get used to calling other members of the club, 'bru'.

We greeted one another by saying, "Howzit bru."

The rest of the people outside the club were known as 'Peasants' and were always referred to as such.

We would meet outside a cafe on Main Street (opposite the old bus terminus), and at that stage we were also divided into different sections. For example: East Rand, Northern Suburbs and Bronx (Hillbrow) section.

Riding through the city centre with no less than 50 motorcycles, was quite an exhilarating experience. The distance between you and the other bikes was minimal and a hazardous speed of approximately 140-160km/h was maintained. If the leader went through a green robot, the whole 'crew' would go through, two of the riders ensuring that the cross traffic was kept at bay, irrespective of whether the robot was red or green.

I found that riding my bike was something I lived for. My whole life revolved around my 'wife'. Work became a waste of time. I visited the doctor in Boksburg more frequently—a week's sick leave here—and two weeks there and, suddenly, I didn't feel like working at all. Every night was spent in Joburg, riding around, taking drugs, 'popping pills', looking for women and now and again, some trouble. One night, I went to buy marijuana from a drug merchant just a little way down the road from 'High Point' in Hillbrow. He was the watchman of a block of flats. That night I met

Jane, a girl from Australia who stayed in the flats and who was also buying a joint. I went with her to her flat and we smoked it up all night till we 'freaked out'.

The next night, she told us she was on a certain tablet, which made her feel high. That night, Nic, his Chinese girlfriend, Jane and I all took an overdose of these tablets. I remember chewing and chewing on my teeth for hours. Jane went and bought bubble gum, which they forced into my mouth so that I would not damage my teeth. We spent days tripping on the pills. For weeks after that, my jaws and teeth were extremely painful, and I struggled to eat.

At my sister's wedding (above).   *Out there riding (above).*

Spending time riding my motorcycle with the 'brotherhood' was a big part of my life, from a very young age. Me left in pic.

Jane asked me to move in with her, which I did, but I used to go to work at least three days a week. The days I did spend at work were bad, as most of the time I was trying to recover from a trip, and I was on a 'heavy downer' sleeping in the toilets or finding a hideaway place on the roof of the factory.

Weekends and Wednesday nights were spent with the crew. A lot of Friday nights were spent at a hotel in Germiston, where a live band played on the first floor. One Friday night, while I was sitting outside on my bike, smoking a joint with Jane, a fight started at the entrance to the hotel.

We saw someone fall to the ground with blood oozing out of his chest from a knife wound.

"Damn!" I shouted to Jane. "It's one of the crew. I must help."

I ran over, lifted the fellow and laid him over the back of a mate's bike and we rushed him to the hospital where they operated immediately. We found out later that the knife had only just missed his heart.

By the time I arrived back at the hotel, another scuffle had started, but this time they had knocked over the crew leader's bike.

I put my bike on its main stand and ran to where two people were embracing in a struggle to get the upper hand of one another. I ran, kicked both men that were on the ground and proceeded to pick up the leader's bike when suddenly, out of the corner of my eye, I saw something coming towards my head. I lifted my arm and felt the pain surge through my body as the blow of a baton crashed onto my arm.

I ran into the street, removing from my leather jacket the set of police handcuffs I always kept on me. With one loop locked around my hand, I lashed out at the two big fellows who had teamed up and were rushing in for the kill, one with a baton and the other with a switch blade. I could feel the crunch of metal against bone and saw blood all over the one's face as the metal handcuff ripped into the side of his face.

The one with the switchblade shouted, "I'll kill you as I did that other bastard crew member."

Ignoring his threats, I charged him with the cuffs, once again feeling the crunch of bone and flesh. I was full of drugs and drink and felt no pity whatsoever. I wanted to kill them both. I knew I could, as I had learned to keep my head in a street fight at a very early age and to fight to kill, not win. Just then, the rest of the crew came running out of the hotel.

"What's happening?" a member shouted.

"They just trashed Ron's bike," I said pointing to the two attackers who had started running down the road as they saw members of the crew come outside.

We ran after them and caught them. Two of us got hold of one. I kept hitting him with the cuffs, as both loops of the cuffs were now wrapped around my hand. He shouted and cried for me to stop, but I felt nothing. His nose, mouth, eyes, and ears were one mass of raw flesh and blood.

Something snapped in me.

"He must die! He must die!" I kept shouting as I lashed at his head and face.

If my mates hadn't stopped me, I probably would not have stopped till he was out. It was as if I had no control over myself. I wanted to see him dead.

I heard someone shouting, "Give me a knife, damn give me a knife. I want to cut the bastard's throat!"

One of my mates wanted to cut up his mate. Suddenly, there were sirens, barking dogs and police all over. I panicked; I didn't know if this fellow I had sorted out was dead or not.

"It's that one with the long blonde hair and beard." I heard coming from the crowds.

I ran for my life and saw a white car waiting for the robot to turn green. I opened the back door, grabbed the driver around the throat, stuck a knife under his throat and told him to ride. He got the fright of his life, put down his foot and we were gone. I told him to ride for fifteen minutes, then to drop me off in the park and to go back and ask one of the crew members to bring my bike. I threatened him if he did not do it, I would trace him by his vehicle's number plate and sort him out. He kept telling me he liked the crew and that he would take care of me. If I ever needed anything, I must contact him.

About half an hour later, one of the crew brought my bike to the park. I was glad to get my 'wife' back again. I had been worried about her. That same night, I shaved off my beard because I was scared the police would trace me.

Everyone would say, "Howzit, Billy the Kid, my mate."

Man, at 19, this was indeed an honour and made me feel good; I felt I had earned a place in the 'crew'. This name was sewn to the bottom of my colours. My general working days were becoming fewer and fewer, and the sick leave was mounting up. I had a warning from my work that my sick leave and vocational leave were completely out of control.

One night, just before leaving a particular pub, a bolt that holds the main stand of my motorcycle broke. The rest of 'the crew' left and two mates stayed to help me. After quite a struggle, I decided to pop in at a mate who stayed in a flat in Hillbrow, Johannesburg. On arriving, I found that there was a heavy drug party going on, couples were lying all over the flat, the smell of marijuana filled the air, and 'heavy music' was coming from all sides.

I was introduced to a lovely girl who seemed out of place with the rest of the crowd. Her name was Candy. She told me she worked at the airport as a hostess and had only just moved into the block of flats. I took the opportunity and asked her if we could be alone. We went to her flat and I asked her if she wanted to make a 'marijuana pipe'. She said no, as she had never taken drugs before. I kept at it all night until she agreed. We smoked a few joints until the early hours of the morning. I had just begun to ruin another life.

I was going downhill full speed and was not concerned who went with me in the process. I decided to leave Jane and move in with Candy. I also decided that my working days were now finished and didn't want to go back to work again. Now I had the full day and night to do all the things I wanted to do. My girlfriend paid my bike instalment every month and supplied finance for our drugs, drinks and fuel for the wife (bike).

There were times when I was so 'slammed' as I rode on my bike that I even prayed to God and asked Him if I was killed that He would forgive me for my sins and take me to heaven. But on reaching my destination, God and all His goodness and holiness were immediately forgotten.

The Bible says in John 9:31, For God heareth not the prayer of a sinner, but He that doeth His will, him He heareth.

I believe the only prayer of a sinner God hears, is the cry for forgiveness of sins and a request for Jesus to enter your life and from then on, He hears all our prayers if we continue to walk in His ways and if we allow Him to be Lord and Master of our lives.

The foundation my parents laid in my life was indeed a good foundation because it was based on the Word of God. I knew there was a God and indeed a heaven, but I also knew there was a Devil and a hell and knew and was afraid that if I got killed, I would go to hell.

I sadly admit that I never really loved Candy, but I used her to satisfy my own selfish needs. Young girls, beware of cheap relationships; look to God for the right man.

One day, Candy said, "Billy, how would you like to have your own children and settle down?"

I looked at her for a long time, wondering if she was going to pop the question, *"Would you like to get married?"*

"What for?" I answered, wanting to get off the subject.

She was quiet for a while, then she said, "I think I'm pregnant."

"Damn you!" I shouted, "You cow, where am I supposed to get money to rear a child? We must get rid of it!"

"No!" she shouted almost hysterically. "No, never!"

"Well then, I'm leaving," I threatened.

"Please, Billy," she pleaded, crying hysterically.

I grabbed my leather jacket, ran outside, jumped on my bike and hit her 'full throttle' in every gear back to Hillbrow. I got some pills, went home late and suggested Candy take them. Both of us went on a 'cheap rave' popping at least four pills each. The next day, we were on downers and two days later, she told me the 'foetus' was lost. I was relieved, but she was in a terrible state. This having happened and being on a downer, she was close to suicide. All I knew was that I was not getting hooked on any 'broad' right now (may God help her to find Him as Lord and Master of her life and to find the grace to forgive me, Oh Lord! How low and evil had I become!).

On more than one occasion, I pawned her radio, hair dryer, earrings, and watch for drugs and fuel money. One night, our neighbours had a party, and as usual, marijuana and pills were freely available. We made a 'hubbly bubbly' with wine and drank the wine afterwards. One of the guests at the party told us quite proudly that she was a high-class prostitute. She was very pretty and had a boyfriend who did not work, so she supported both.

She began to tell us of her many encounters with customers at a very well-known five-star hotel in Johannesburg. Her boyfriend sat next to her as she told us how some men beat her up and refused to pay her for services rendered. Her daily salary was astronomical. I remember her telling us that when she finally got home, she felt dirty and used and she would scrub herself, sometimes till she bled, yet she felt continuously dirty and could not overcome that feeling.

My thoughts went back to the days when I felt clean, looked clean and was clean, inside and out. My brothers and I used to play church. We even used to fight about whose turn it was to preach. The other two would then have to sit in the congregation and listen and when the offering plate came their way, they would have to give the small change they have collected from other family members.

On our way to church. My dearest dad (back), and twin brothers on either side of me.

Reflecting on the tumultuous path that I chose and that has subsequently unfolded since my childhood, I am confronted with the massive toll it took—both on myself and those around me.

Especially my parents, with deep hopes and dreams for us, their children, bore witness to the sombre reality that engulfed my life by the age of 20.

In the depths of despair, even my very countenance (below) spoke volumes of the darkness and emptiness that consumed me.

I recall a verse from the Bible:

John 10:10: The thief (the Devil) comes only to steal, kill, and destroy; I have come that you may have life, and have it to the full.

Somehow, the deception of the world overwrites any goodness that God desires for your life if you allow it. The very choices you make in your life you will have to give an answer to the Almighty God. (Ecclesiastes 11:9)

CHAPTER 6

FURTHER INTO THE GUTTER

The beat of the music filled the whole block of flats. It was party time again and I found myself in a flat in Hillbrow, drugged up and swaying to the music with a girl in my arms.

"Billy!" someone was shouting at the top of his voice. It was Nic. "I want you to meet a mate," he continued shouting. "His name is Reg."

I thrust out my hand.

"Howzit Reg," I said.

Reg was later to become the leader of a gang that specialised in robberies.

I had lost the job I had at the military aircraft manufacturer in South Africa, even though I had completed almost three years of apprenticeship training. Now only 19 and unable to keep a steady job. So, my days were filled with looking for ways and means to get money. Nic, Reg and I spent more and more time together.

Reg's father was into horse racing. So many of our Wednesdays and Saturdays were spent at the track betting on horses with money received from stolen items we pawned. The only problem was that there was never enough money.

One day, Reg's father told us that he had a good plan to get lots of money. We were to rob a large shop in Vereeniging, a town not too far from Johannesburg. It was their 'month end' and the safe would be full of money. His dad had managed to get inside information and the plan was as follows:

After closing time, at 5pm, the four of us (two from Reg's crew, together with Nic and myself), armed with knives, rope and batons, would enter the shop (According to his informant, he would ensure that the shop would not be locked at the time given for us to 'whack' the shop).

The shop manager, together with two assistants, would be doing stocktaking. Reg's father said he would sit in the getaway car with a .38 revolver, which he would keep in case there was trouble. We pleaded with him, telling him it would go much quicker if we kept the gun, but he refused. Well, everything went according to plan; the door was closed but not locked, and all four of us walked in. I remember clutching the knife handle in my pocket, wondering if I would have to use it.

The minute we entered, we walked towards what seemed like an office. As we passed a high shoe rack, out of the corner of my eye, I saw movement. It was two assistants and in front of us was the manager plus two more assistants. We were outnumbered. I wondered if we should turn and run or fight it out. We didn't have the revolver and by the look on their faces, I knew they knew something was going to go down. A deadly silence filled the entire shop, and everyone just stared at each other after what seemed to be an hour (in reality, a few seconds). Reg broke the silence with a loud question:

"Hey, which way is it to the hotel?"

Relieved, the manager came forward.

"Look," he said. "My shop is closed."

He took us outside and showed us the way to the hotel. We were really upset because we had already planned what we were going to do with all the money and goods we were going to get.

Disappointed, we returned to Johannesburg. However, having started this hard-core theft, we were constantly looking for ways to get money. Shops and banks were scrutinised as possible opportunities to get money. I saw the wonderful things everyone who worked hard had, but

I was not prepared to work. I wanted shortcuts to getting these things and the only alternative was through stealing. This is what I convinced myself of every day.

About a week later, Reg's dad told us to get our weapons together. We were going to pull a job at a bank in town. He seemed drugged up and we were a little wary, but we went along with him anyway. This was going to be a recce trip (reconnaissance). To our surprise, we turned into a basement garage parking area but were stopped by a security guard and a chain across the entrance. Reg's father greeted the guard, the chain was dropped and in we went. Once in the basement, we got into a lift and the button indicating the first floor was pressed.

The lift stopped, the doors opened, we walked out, and believe it or not, we were standing behind the bank tellers. I couldn't believe my eyes. Suddenly, the bank became quiet, and everybody looked at us. It was too late; we weren't prepared. We all walked out of the front door, leaving the whole bank utterly astonished. We ran around the block and hid in a shop while my friend's father fetched the car and picked us up.

Every day was spent drugged up and thinking about ways to steal money. Nic and I made sure each time we were involved in a robbery that there was no connection between us and the crew we were riding for at that stage. On one occasion, at about 12 at night, we were on our way, with Reg's crew, to the home of the managing director of a big shopping complex. We were going to hold his wife hostage while we forced him to give us money and take us to the different shops for clothes, etc. But we needed more weapons. We tried to buy guns on the 'black market' but didn't even have enough money for that. We were becoming more and more desperate.

Candy had become very concerned about all my doings and told me that she couldn't go out with me when the possibility was constantly there that I would end up in jail or, worse, killed. I decided to 'cool it' a bit, as I was completely dependent on her for paying for my motorcycle and a place to sleep. The little financial support I was getting, I got from her (may our Lord Jesus bless this lady with great salvation).

I must say, with all these things happening, I was becoming more and more empty inside. The longing for inner peace and stability became greater, yet there seemed to be no light at the end of this very dark tunnel.

My thoughts often went back to my childhood days, when the whole family would go to church. I had really loved Jesus and used to get excited when it was time to go to church. Dad and Mom taught us that the most important thing in our lives must be our relationship with the living God.

I did not want to ponder on these thoughts too long because I knew they were good, real and the only way—but not for me, not just yet, I would tell myself.

Hillbrow used to come alive after 9:30pm and by midnight, a place called 'High Point' was the centre of attraction. All kinds of people made their way here to meet others or to get something to eat. We spent a lot of our time sitting on our motorcycles, watching the people. We were not allowed to wear our colours in Hillbrow, so the denim jackets with crew emblems were worn under our leather jackets.

One night, while I was lying on my bike with my head on the headlamp and my feet on the rear crash bar, I heard a lot of 'cat whistles'. Looking up, I saw a young man, about 30 years old, clean-shaven, with two beautiful girls who wore normal dresses, not micro miniskirts, as was the norm in those years. They both beamed with beauty. I had seen sexier and more attractive girls, but these had a beauty and cleanliness I find hard to explain.

I felt myself, for the first time, envying another man. Here I was with my long, shoulder-length hair (filled with knots and split ends from the wind) and 'original jeans' that had not been washed in years. I seriously looked and felt like a bedraggled piece of humanity. The man had a guitar and amplifier and suddenly they began to sing about Jesus. Deep, deep inside, there was a cut. I knew this was so good, yet I wanted to get away.

When I heard the name of Jesus, my thoughts flashed back to when I was 11 years old and had become very ill with rheumatic fever (all my joints went stiff), and I asked my dad to take me to the minister's house so that they could pray for me. I was anointed with oil and prayed for. The next morning, when I opened my eyes, I knew Jesus had healed me; my stiff joints were as good as new.

I jumped out of bed and screamed, "Mom, Dad, Jesus has healed me; I'm well! Look, I can walk and move my hands! Yahoo!"

I ran outside shouting, "Thank you, Jesus!"

I don't know what the neighbours thought, and I didn't care.

Church became something of greater value to me at such a young age. I really loved Jesus and desired to walk closely with Him.

Off to church at the age of 11. I'm on the right and my twin brothers on the left of me.

I was jerked back to reality by the thundering revving of motorcycles. It was Nic and Al who had started their bikes and were revving it up as if they were about to 'throw a doughnut' (round tar burn with the back wheel of the motorcycle) right there at Highpoint in Hillbrow, with exceptional exhaust systems on the 4-cylinder beasts; everybody was looking at us now and people came running to see what was happening. The three people never stopped singing, but you could not hear anything.

I immediately jumped off my bike and turned off their motorcycles. They were just about to make a scene when we realised everyone was watching us and we were supposed to be 'brothers'. I told them we should 'split', which we did, making as much racket as we could when we left.

I will never forget that group – only three of them – but their courage was way more than that of all of us standing around. To be honest, in the depths of my heart, I couldn't help but feel a twinge of envy at their purity and sobriety. Oh, how I yearned for their sanctity and may I say it, 'Holiness'.

CHAPTER 7

HIT THE ROAD

With the busy traffic of the city now behind, it was the open road that lay ahead. Tucked behind those clip-on handlebars, one arm resting on the tank and Nic crouched in behind me, preparing a marijuana pipe 'laced' with mandrax, all I could hear was the comforting, thundering sound of the Iron Lady, who knew what she wanted. She kept asking for more through her four straight-through cylinders. My hand turned the throttle almost viciously in response to her cry. The rev counter needle was now already in the red, and the speedo needle was moving to the 200+km point. If only I could get more. I moved closer to the tank and felt Nic respond almost instinctively—the needle moved a fraction. If I could only get more, this had to be a record run.

Trees and bushes alongside the road had now become only blurred images, with the wind distorting every part of my face. It seemed as if the cars had come to a standstill as we flew past at some 210km per hour.

Suddenly, a nudge in my back and a shout in the ear from Nic.

"Make a pipe, bru!"

He would pass me a small clay pipe known as a *'jalompie'*. Without slowing down, I would take a few pulls and push the Iron Lady even further. This was one of our regular record-breaking trips from Joburg to Durban on the East Coast. The record we held was four and a half hours to do some 580km. I wonder if we realised that death was an extra passenger on all of those runs, just waiting to bring us in.

Nic and I often took a trip to Durban, usually to get a good supply of 'Durban Poison' marijuana (when finances were available). We would normally ride two-up on his 750 KO 4-cylinder Honda; each one would get a turn to rest and make a few marijuana pipes laced with mandrax while the other rode. The average speed was in the region of 200 to 210km per hour (speedometer speed). On one occasion, we had rain from Mooi River to Durban. We weren't great believers in rain suits or even luggage, for that matter; we believed in 'go as you are'.

On arriving in Durban at 11 at night, we were drenched, hungry and tired. Our first priority was to get a place to sleep. Within an hour, we had shacked up with a group of druggies from Durban. About four couples were staying in a one-bedroom flat. They loaned us some dry clothes and we were off to get some food. We only had enough money to buy drugs. There was not even enough money for petrol to get us home.

While on the main beachfront area, I noticed an old homeless man who had just received money to buy some KFC chicken. He also had a small parcel with him, so I decided to follow him at a distance. It wasn't long before he turned into a back alley. I told Nic we must attack him and take his food. We walked up behind him. I grabbed him around the neck and held the knife to his throat while Nic grabbed his parcel of chicken.

He got such a fright that he jerked loose and screamed at the top of his voice as he ran down the alley, "Help! Watchman! Help! Watchman!"

We went through the rest of his belongings, only to find a Bible. Seeing the well-used Bible, I knew that this man knew God. I felt bad because of what I had done and feared that God would punish me. I threw all his belongings onto the ground, grabbed the grilled chicken, and ran.

The next day we went down to the beach in our wet clothes, took them all off, laid them in the sun and lay in the sun in our underpants.

It wasn't long before we heard someone calling, "Make a pipe!"

It was a young Indian man who was selling cold beers, but in his left hand he had a pipe made from a bottle neck with marijuana and mandrax mixed. He gave us a few pulls on the pipe and asked us if we were interested in buying mandrax and DP (Durban Poison). We said yes and agreed to meet him at a well-known hotel on the beachfront the next day.

Later that day, one of the group of people we were staying with came and told us about a young schoolboy with very rich parents who was staying in a hotel. One of the girls in the group we connected with was a so-called 'nymphomaniac', and the rich, young schoolboy had offered her a lot of money for sex. She agreed to meet him at the flat where we were staying and arranged for us to 'rip off' his hotel room while she kept him busy.

When we got to his room, we broke in and found a few hundred rands worth of traveller's cheques in a leather holder. In the front of the cheque book was a cheque with his signature on it. We immediately forged the signature on the rest of the cheques and looked for a place to cash them. The first was a well-known restaurant on West Street. We had a good meal, paid with the cheque, and got change in cash. We carried on at bars, cafes, and restaurants.

The next day, we bought marijuana and mandrax and financed a wild party at the flat. Two nights later, we had just finished smoking marijuana on the beach when a police squad car pulled in. A constable and a police sergeant jumped out of the car and immediately smelled my hand and told us we had just smoked marijuana. I admitted it, as I knew there was no use in denying it. They searched us both and the bike but could find nothing. All they found was the top of the bottle neck, which we had used to smoke the marijuana. He told us they could lock us up on suspicion for 90 days (I don't know how true it was), but he gave us twelve hours to get out of Durban and told us that after 12 hours, every squad car in Durban would be looking for us. We decided to leave early the next morning. That night, we slept in the bowls club behind the Marine Parade.

Around this time, a friend of ours was given a jail sentence for a serious crime he had committed. His wife and child stayed in a flat and we used to go and visit her, smoke it up and just chat in general. One night, we got onto the subject of Satan worship, and she told us that she and her husband were deep into the occult. She told us that she could help us sell our souls in exchange for many things and she told us about very wealthy and well-known people in Johannesburg who had sold their souls in exchange for wealth and other desires. She also told us about visits from evil spirits. That night we stayed there, but I could not sleep; something felt evil and out of place.

Candy, my girlfriend, had now moved to Kempton Park to be closer to the airport where she worked. One night, after a crew meeting, about six of us were riding home on the main highway from Johannesburg when one of the motorcycles ran out of fuel. We removed the petrol tank from the one motorcycle, held the fuel tap over the empty tank and gave him enough fuel to get home. On arriving at

Candy's flat, I knocked and knocked but got no answer. I tried to open the door with my key, but it was locked from the inside with the key still in the lock. I realised she was home, but something was wrong when the door burst open and there she was, as pale as could be, shaking like a leaf. I thought maybe I had arrived at an 'inconvenient' time and asked her if there was someone in the flat.

"No!" she insisted. "I've been astro travelling."

I hadn't the faintest idea what she was talking about, so she began telling me how she had seen me giving fuel to a friend from a tank we had removed from one motorcycle, holding it over another motorcycle's tank.

She told me who all had been present around the motorcycles on the side of the highway. I asked her if she had been to Johannesburg and passed us on the way and she went on to explain the whole (Devilish) matter. I was then invited to try it, which I did, but to no avail. I concentrated a little harder, but nothing.

"Have you at any time in your life been a Christian and committed your life to Jesus?" Candy asked.

"Yes," I answered, rather surprised at the question.

To my amazement, she said, "That's why. It will never work if you have accepted Christ as there must be a complete giving over of oneself to an external spiritual force." (evil, wicked).

My warning to young people is to be careful with the 'innocent things' you so easily get involved in. It's a trap; once you are in, there is no getting out. Only Christ can bring satisfaction and joy to your ever enquiring mind.

Our drug merchant in Hillbrow was caught by the narcotic squad, so we were on the lookout for a new supplier. We had other suppliers but quite a distance to travel in order to get 'good quality drugs' and not *menjat* (bad quality).

We were buying good marijuana from a young lady in Mayfair (a suburb of Johannesburg). One day, she introduced us to her friend. We were invited across the road to 'make a few pipes' with her and her husband. We accepted the invitation and went across.

The whole family was into drugs. This included the grandfather, who showed us newspaper clippings of himself having been in prison no less than fifty times for dealing in drugs; the grandmother, who was on some heavy pills and the sister and her boyfriend, who had been 'pushing needle' and had been tripping for quite a few days already.

They were lying on the bed, oblivious to Nic and myself in the doorway, as we were introduced. Her husband was a well-known Mayfair gangster who had big yellow and black stains on his hands from smoking marijuana—the bigger the stain, the bigger the gangster, they believed. The entire family stayed in a small, semi-detached house and the little money they received came from welfare organisations.

We went to the back of the house, where they had a full-size woman's face and body engraved on the wall. This was an old drug addict's way of smoking marijuana. With a mouthful of water, smoke is inhaled through the water in your mouth, then the smoke and water are blown against the wall, specifically at the woman's mouth, where it runs down the centre of the engraved body and bubbles form at the bottom of the floor at her feet, forming a small puddle of water. We had been 'blowing chaurner' for quite some time when a young boy, not older than three years I imagine, with amazing long blonde hair and blue eyes came around the corner and asked me in Afrikaans if I would put him on my bike. I immediately agreed and picked him up, but his mother interrupted and asked him if he didn't want to take a quick 'pull' from the marijuana pipe. He took about three long 'drags', till his eyes went all glassy and he sat down, mumbling words and asking for more. Of course, everybody broke out in laughter, but, deep in my soul, I was hurting and thought about my young brother back home, probably a little older but who was raised in such a wonderful, loving and God-fearing home.

My thoughts also drifted to the excellent Christian upbringing I had. My parents were not just Sunday Christians, but everyday Christians who loved the Lord Jesus and constantly showed us by way of example the right road to take. They showed their love to us as children, not only with gifts and nice things, but with the greatest gift they could give us: Jesus, the Son of God, the gift they had so freely received. I hated watching this young kid so 'drugged up' and immediately picked him up again, took him to my bike and we went for a long ride.

After that, we played pinball (I was totally addicted to playing pinball machines) at a shop. Over the months, I continued to visit that family regularly and had a soft spot for this young boy. Today, I wonder where he is. Maybe he is in jail or, like his father, caught up in one of the many street gangs, but one thing I know, that without the Lord Jesus, he is lost in a very, very dark world and is without hope. My Lord Jesus, please have mercy on his life as you did with mine, as I believe with all my heart that nothing is impossible with God and Jesus will not easily give up on you.

I thank the Lord daily for my praying parents and a church that was committed to praying for me and my brothers.

CHAPTER 8

THE FINAL 'JOL'

"Billy, let's make this one of the greatest 'jols' we've ever had, bru! Like something to remember, man!" Nic said as he slowly took a long pull from a 'joint'.

"Ja bru, like a jol we can tell our kids about one day,"

I answered thinking of the big motorcycle rally (Dassie Rally) happening on the Easter weekend in Bulawayo, Zimbabwe.

Preparations were in full swing; our passports were all in order, but I desperately needed money. Candy, my girlfriend, did give me some money, but I needed more (always needed more). This was going to be five days of non-stop biking, beers, women, drugs and action, so I started stealing post from private post-boxes at hundreds of residential flats in Hillbrow, Johannesburg.

I would steal the post, put it in a bag, ride to a lonely spot and open thousands upon thousands of envelopes with letters, sometimes finding money, other times cheques and most of the time nothing valuable. This went on for quite a few weeks before the rally.

One morning, I took Candy to work and decided to pop in to visit a bru in Hillbrow who stayed in the penthouse suite opposite the hospital. I left my motorcycle on the pavement outside the entrance to the flats and took a lift to the penthouse suite. My mate and I were busy chatting when I heard a motorcycle start up and recognised the sound; it sounded like my bike was being started by someone. We both rushed to the balcony but could see nothing, so we rushed down to investigate. The minute I got outside the block of flats, I realised that my bike was stolen.

"Damn, someone stole my wife!" I shouted, running up and down the pavement like a madman. I ran across the road and grabbed a watchman sitting at the entrance to the hospital.

"Did you see my bike? Who stole it? Talk, you bastard!" I was shouting and shaking this poor man around like I was a madman.

"No! Stop! I saw no one!" he answered, terrified.

"Stop! Stop!" It was my mate who brought me back to reality again.

"Stop, bru! Stop, you idiot! He knows nothing; we'll find it," Nic reassured me.

We phoned the police, who took a statement and said I would have to wait six weeks before the insurance would pay out. The chances of finding my 'wife' looked poor; this was Johannesburg.

My whole dream had crumbled. I thought of the motorcycle rally that was coming up in Zimbabwe and the crew I was now riding with. I was nothing without my 'wife.' I needed her so badly! I cursed everyone and God for allowing this to happen. We considered stealing a motorcycle. Nic and I discussed it in detail and decided to first check out a few people we knew who steal anything and everything for a living. The next two days were spent riding from one thief gang to another, but without success. They knew nothing of her. I suspected the leader of a certain gang that we knew well had set this up, as he knew my every movement.

"Hey Billy, don't '*sig*' (worry), my mate," Nic said. "We'll steal you a beauty when we come back from Zimbabwe."

"I'm going to whip a new bike out of a shop," I said. "No second-hand trash and if the cops catch me, at least it will be worth it," I added, not caring a damn any more as I was like a bird without wings.

So Nic and I decided to go 'two-up' to Zimbabwe to the famous Dassie Rally just outside the town of Bulawayo.

This way, we would also have more money to spend on booze and marijuana.

The Sunday night before the rally, we were at the crew meeting in the boxing club, discussing the travelling and other arrangements. The crew leader told us if any of the crew was killed in an accident, we would return to South Africa immediately. We all laughed, saying none of us would 'come short'. We were also asked not to leave in convoy from Johannesburg but in small groups at staggered times and we would meet at Louis Trichardt, where the police made their barracks available for us to sleep the night.

I had bought a lot of marijuana from Swaziland and two bottles of brandy for the journey. We left in a group of about 12 motorcycles. Our average speed was approximately 140-160km per hour. The traffic was heavy because it was Easter weekend. Every 50 kilometres or so, a few of us would stop to have some brandy and smoke marijuana. At about 12 that night, we went over a speed trap just before the town of Louis Trichardt, doing some 180+km per hour.

We were stopped and asked to ride carefully. We arrived in the town just after midnight and slept at the police barracks that night (with all my 'marijuana stash' safely tucked away under the seat of the motorcycle). Early the next morning, we were on our way to the border post. When we got to Beitbridge (border post), there were thousands of people going into Zimbabwe for the long weekend. I had hidden some of our marijuana stash in my crash helmet, which most of us had now taken off because, at that stage, there were no crash helmet laws in Zimbabwe.

We quickly went through immigration and customs and were on our way to the city of Bulawayo. There were about 130 motorcycles, with a lot of the guys riding 'two-up' to save on costs. On arriving in Bulawayo, we were greeted by television crews and hundreds of people eager to get a glimpse of the motorcycles and the crazy people riding them. Some of us really looked quite a sight, as this was also the hippy era. Nic and I were in a continuous drunken and drugged state, having smoked marijuana and boozing all the way to Zimbabwe.

"Come on, Nic," I shouted. "The crew is leaving for the campsite!"

We were camped some 24 kilometres outside Bulawayo, and it was Saturday morning. Everyone was waiting for the big 'jol' in town at the nightclubs.

Nic and I did exactly as we had planned; not one moment went by that we were not boozing, drinking, smoking marijuana and popping pills.

It was 5pm that afternoon and the clubs had closed until later in the evening, when they would reopen. I was exiting the club in a really bad state, began to cross the main road to meet up with Nic and the motorcycle when suddenly, everything went blank. Then I heard people talking, strange remarks and wondered who they were talking about. As I opened my eyes, I saw what looked like hundreds of faces looming over me. I was, in fact, lying flat on my back on the ground in the middle of the road. A car had knocked me over while crossing the street.

"Look, his eyes are opening!" someone shouted.

Oh no! I thought to myself. *Am I dead or going mad?* I turned my head to see that I was half-lying against a car in the middle of the road. I tried to stand, but my leg was hurting badly. I held onto the car and looked in. A man, woman and a small child were in the car and looked terrified. Suddenly, the car pulled out from under me, and I fell down again.

"Shoot the bastard!" I heard someone from the crew scream.

"Let's get him!" more shouts. By now there were motor-cycles starting, chains swinging and shouts of, "Let's get them!"

Well, it seemed like just a few minutes later they all came back, only to report that they could not catch the guy. Somehow, the family managed to get away, and I am glad that they did.

I was taken to the hospital, where they took X-rays and told me I had cracked a bone in my leg.

The minute it happened, I had a weird feeling that God was going to get me. Then, everything became clear—first my motorcycle was stolen and now I had had this accident—I was terrified. Sitting in the hospital, these thoughts racing through my head, I heard a funny noise and giggles from behind the emergency room screens.

"Sst, ssst, sssst."

I got up and hobbled on one leg to look behind the screens, only to find two nurses spraying deodorant under the screen due to my feet stinking so badly; I hadn't washed for five days or removed my riding boots during that time at all.

"Hey, Peasant," (what we called non-crew members), I said under my breath. "Get on with the job and forget the jam!" I rudely shouted to the nurses.

My leg was bandaged up, and we returned to the camp just outside of Bulawayo. I tried to find other means to get back to South Africa, as I was terrified to go back by motorcycle. That same night, the leader returned to camp and told us that one of the crew had been killed when his bike had left the road. A hush came over us; this was now a 'sig' (worry/fear). I was now more determined than ever to get a lift by car, if I could.

Fortunately, I managed to get a lift home with one of the crew members in his Volkswagen Beetle. As we were driving, we were drinking bottles of wine, which he seemed to have an endless supply of.

On arriving back at my girlfriend's flat in Johannesburg, she fussed all over me, wanting to know what had happened.

"My darling, I was so worried about you," Candy cried as she embraced me and held me tightly to herself. "You're back at last." Then she released me abruptly.

"Billy, you must phone your sister urgently in connection with your father," she said, looking to see how I would react, knowing of the conflict between my father and myself.

Something happened inside my stomach—a sort of sickening feeling. "Dad, oh Dad, please don't be dead or sick." I found myself crying within myself. "God, first my bike, now my father. Please be merciful."

"Billy, Billy, don't worry! I don't think it's serious," Candy said in her soft, almost gentle voice, startled by my terrified reaction.

I ran and phoned my sister immediately.

"Hi Jen, what's wrong with Dad?" I asked immediately.

"No, Bill, he's fine; he just wants to see you at the Johannesburg airport when he comes back from Cape Town," she answered. This was probably a white lie because my dad never really wanted to see me again, the feeling being mutual.

But God had a plan. We met each other at the airport.

I must have looked like a terrible mess with my leather jacket, dirty 'originals' (denim jeans that had not been washed in five or six years), a 'hop along' leg, long hair and a beard that had been growing for years.

I expected him to curse me and chase me away, but instead, in front of all the people, he put out his arms, embraced me and his first words were:

"Hello, my boy! Won't you come home, son? We all love you."

My sister, father and I sat at a nearby roadhouse and spoke for a while. It was then that I decided to tell Candy that I was leaving her to try and sort out the mess my life was currently in.

When I told her about my dad's offer, she was very upset and would not speak to me for quite a few days.

I wondered if she was pregnant again, but she kept reassuring me that she was not. After a week, I said goodbye to Candy and left.

By now, I had no job, no hope and no future. Once I got home, I tried hundreds of places to try to finish my apprenticeship, but they would tell me to wait a day or two and then on my return, they would apologise and say, sorry, no vacancies. The apprentice board in South Africa had marked me (and rightly so) as a deserter and unreliable, a drug addict, thief, and motorcycle gang member. Overall, they said I was bad news. I only discovered this much later on, when my life was beginning to change.

It wasn't long, and I was back with my old friends in my old town, boozing and taking drugs. One day, I took some money that I had stolen and gambled it on a horse race at the renowned July Handicap held in Durban, South Africa. Believe it or not, I won R1350 (approximately $75).

To celebrate, Don and I sat in the bar and drank double whiskies one after the other. I decided after some time that I needed fresh air. I walked outside of the hotel and leaned against a stop sign at the corner of the road. It spun around and I realised it was loose in a pipe in the ground. So, I removed the sign (for some unknown reason) and laid it at an angle against the wall of the hotel.

Don came out of the bar, swaying from side to side, slammed, of course. He took a long look at the stop sign, then, without warning, pulled his head back, rushed forward and hit his face 'head on' with all his might against the brick wall. Turning around, half-dazed, he looked at me and started laughing. I took one look at Don's face; his nose was bleeding profusely; above his eyes were two large gashes with blood running down them; his teeth, top and bottom, had cut through his lips and blood was running out of his mouth.

I stood for a while and looked at him and I shouted, "I'm done; this is madness! What has become of us? I'm never touching booze again." I never wanted to taste alcohol again and made up my mind to stop this drinking.

I was unable to find a job, so my father borrowed money from his boss to enable me to finish my studies at technical college. I was determined to make a success but could still not resist taking drugs and marijuana with friends.

Early one Saturday morning, sitting up in bed, alert, I asked my brothers, "Hey guys, you hear something?"

"No, what do you hear?" they answered.

"A bike with no baffles!" I shouted excitedly.

"Straight through exhausts, bru."

"This can only mean one thing: a brother from the crew paying me a visit."

Since I had returned home, I had stopped meeting with the crew. So I had to go to the bottom of my cupboard and haul out my 'ories' (original Levi's), never washed, slipped them on and donned my faithful old leather jacket. I ran outside and waited. I could still hear the bike revving it up as he changed gear. About five minutes later, I see a Honda 750cc. I was right; it was Nic, my old bro.

"Howzit, Billy the kid, my Broer!" Nic shouted above the sound of his bike.

"Howzit Broer!" I answered, slapping his hand.

"You wanna come along to the 'Sat circus' hangout?" Nic invited, knowing there was no way I would say no.

"Hell yea, you know how badly I need a jol, my brother!" I answered, already heading towards his motorcycle.

This gang hangout was located on a farm near the town of

Vereeniging. Most of the gang consisted of young run-aways, both guys and girls. They spent most of their days taking drugs, having sex and planning robberies. I wasn't too happy about going to see them, as I still suspected they had stolen my motorcycle.

When we arrived, there was a big welcome and we were immediately invited to join them to 'rip off' a bottle store on the main road, not too far from the farm.

There were about fifteen young folk on a truck, and we all just invaded the bottle store. While one of the girls bought a bottle of drink, the rest of us packed booze in our pants, jackets, and bags. It all happened so quickly! Before the owners knew what happened, we were out the shop.

Back at the farm, everybody emptied their jackets, pants and pockets. There was enough drink to keep an army drunk for at least a week. I had stopped drinking, so I spent the day smoking pot mixed with mandrax tablets. One of the leaders of the gang decided to slaughter a sheep, so we all ended up chasing a poor sheep around the farm to 'braai' on a spit. Once caught, we cut its throat, and everybody laughed as it tried to walk with blood oozing out of its throat. Soon, the poor animal was skinned and cut up for the barbeque.

"Nic, stop it, you bastard! Help, please! Will someone please help!"

We all heard the girl's screams at the same time. Everyone was looking at me now and waiting for some kind of response.

To hell with you lot, I thought to myself. They ripped off my bike, now Nic can rip off their woman.

The screams came again, and I could hear Nic laughing quite loudly now.

Suddenly, there was silence and then a single shout from Nic, "Billy, my bru!"

This was a frantic call, and I knew straight away there was trouble coming and ran to where the noises were, at the same time feeling in the side of my boot for my flick knife. As I walked into the room two of the Sat gang members were now standing over where Nic and the girl were lying half-clothed on the floor. I pushed the button on my 4-inch flick knife, and she opened with a loud 'click'. The two fellows spun around to focus their attention on the new threat.

"You boys want to spoil Nic's fun?" I asked. "Go ahead and try," I said without waiting for an answer.

By this time, Nic had got his pants on and was groping for his knife.

"Come on, now we are even numbers!" Nic shouted invitingly.

Suddenly, Reg appeared. "Okay, okay, cool it, you guys. Let's have some peace," Reg interrupted.

"Why don't you guys split?" Reg added.

"What for?" Nic answered. "I was just beginning to enjoy it here."

We threatened to burn down their farm and bring reinforcements, if necessary, if Reg interfered. Reg again asked us nicely if we would leave. We told him what we thought of him and his so-called gang and left.

Somehow, those fast days of women, drugs, fighting and motorcycles did not have the same effect on me now that I was back home. Something was different. The vacuum and empty feeling deep inside me were just getting bigger and bigger. Looking back now, I do believe those powerful prayers of my family and the church were taking effect.

I was successful in my studies but was still desperately in need of a job. Some friends told me about the good money they were making working on a new construction site in a small town some 350km from Johannesburg, i.e. Newcastle, which is in the province of Kwa Zulu Natal. One Sunday night, I decided to accompany them to this place called Newcastle (I had never been there before). So, I borrowed a pair of pants, a jacket and a tie from my brother for the interview if there was to be one and with R1.30 ($0.07) in my pocket, enough to buy a carton of milk. Absolutely nothing else. I had ideas of making big money while working on construction, buying another motorcycle and getting back to the crew.

It was 1975, and I was 20. So much had already happened this year. *How was this year going to end?* I thought to myself.

The first night, I joined my two mates in their hostel room and slept on the floor; their hostel was specifically built for the construction teams. Early next morning, I got dressed and accompanied them to work to meet their foreman; however, on the way to work, we passed a building where a lot of people were standing outside, clothed in overalls and it seemed they were waiting for the gates to open.

I asked my friends what place that was, and they told me it was the apprentice training centre.

"Hey guys," I shouted.

"Please turn back and drop me off at that apprentice training centre."

They agreed, but gave me a dumb look. I was really wanting to find out if I could finish my apprenticeship as I had already done it for a few years.

Once we got to the place, we argued for a while, and they left. I asked the receptionist if it was possible to talk to someone about completing my apprenticeship, as I'd already done it for a few years. She told me to wait, which I did.

Strangely, while waiting, I whispered a prayer, something I had not done for years except when I was concerned that I was going to die in a fight or on a motorcycle in a drugged and drunken state. My prayer was that God would help me get the job and if He did, a promise was made that I would give Him one tenth of my salary every month. Wow! Where did that come from? From my upbringing, I knew about tithing from a very young age, as I was raised in a good Christian home.

Well, the interview seemed to go quite well, and they asked me to return in two days as they had to check on some of my credentials etc.

"Oh no!" I said under my breath, knowing that I had tried this so many times to try and complete my apprenticeship, but each time it would be the same answer from the apprentice board. I walked out of the office and down the road, feeling really lost and without hope of any kind of future. Then, for some strange reason, I remembered the prayer and hoped for the best.

Two days later, I returned without any expectation and to be honest it was really embarrassing. The lady handed me a sealed envelope, thanking her I went outside and sat down on the grass to read the letter inside.

It read, *You can continue with your apprenticeship; however, you will have to start as a first-year apprentice once again.*

So, the three years I had already completed were not recognised for 'some or other' reason.

I remember walking back to the construction hostel to think about this, not liking the idea at all but realising this may be the only chance I was going to receive to get my life back in some kind of order.

It came to me like a light bulb had just been switched on, and I decided it was now or never to start over, so I walked back to the apprentice training centre. To be honest, this time it was more of a sprint just in case they changed their minds.

At the desk, I looked the lady straight in the eyes and said, "Okay, you win. I'll start over!" I blurted it out, surprising even myself.

The forms were signed, and it began all over again.

I worked exceptionally hard (this time around) as an apprentice but was still smoking marijuana and taking drugs with Don and Jack, who were working on the construction site.

One day, while we were smoking marijuana in the room, I popped into the bathroom and while there, I suddenly noticed that the white wall tiles were turning into thick red blood. My arms, feet and hands started turning into the same thick red blood. I thought I was dying and shouted out.

"No, God! Please don't let me die. No, not now, please!" I shouted loudly, even scaring myself and ran to Don's room.

"I'm finished, Don!" I shouted as I threw open his bedroom door. Don was reading the newspaper. He got a fright and looked up at me, eyes wide open.

"What the hell are you talking about?" Don said with a startled look on his face.

"I'm finished with this whole drug scene, marijuana, acid, mandrax, you name it—the whole works. It's over for good," I said.

Don said, laughing, "Bru, I've heard that one before. You've just had a 'paranoia'," he added, almost killing himself with laughter.

However, I was determined never to touch the stuff again, and by the grace of God, I haven't touched the weed or any drugs since that day; it's been 49 years as I write.

I had no money, soap, or toothpaste. In the early morning, I would listen to the showers. When they were turned off, I would wait a few minutes, then sneak in to see if I could find small pieces of soap or maybe an empty toothpaste tube somebody may have left as it was not worth using. On some nights, I was even searching through the hostel dustbins for old tubes of toothpaste.

How low I had gone! This is exactly what the Devil will do with your life, because Jesus said in the Bible:

> *The thief (Devil) comes only to steal, kill*
> *and destroy; I have come that you may*
> *have life and have it to the full.*
> *(John 10:10)*

However, for me, it was my saving grace just to have a decent wash, clean teeth and good breath. Today I appreciate every bar of soap and every tube of toothpaste I use, knowing that they do not just appear in the bathroom.

At this point, I had lost the little I had, so not having an alarm clock made it difficult to wake up for work each morning.

The only way to wake up, was to sleep with the curtains open throughout the night and as soon as it got light, which was any time from 5am on, I would wake up.

I had brought a small packet of tobacco with me from Johannesburg and used to roll my own cigarettes with whatever paper I could find each morning.

Finally, the end of the first month of work had arrived. With great excitement, I set off to the shops, and, of course, at the top of my shopping list were soap and toothpaste, not to mention, an alarm clock.

Something I was not going to forget was my commitment to God to pay a tithe (tenth of my salary) to the church if He got me the job. So, not being part of a church just yet, I would send via the post office a 'tenth' of my salary to my sister, for her to pay into her local church.

By the grace of God, I have been able to pay tithes since that day. Here and there, I may have missed a month, but for me, it was a promise and a commitment I made to God, which I desperately wanted to keep.

The first Sunday morning after I got the job, I asked Jack to take me to church in the main town, some 10km from the hostel. He said he wouldn't mind going with me. We had no idea which church to go to, so we stopped outside the Anglican Church as it was quite early in the morning and there were already a few cars parked outside.

I'll never forget what was preached that morning. It was certainly not coincidental that the priest spoke about giving to God what is God's and giving to Caesar what is his. I immediately saw the connection with paying a portion of my salary each month and knew that this was God confirming to me that I had made a promise to Him and He had kept His side of the bargain (if I can call it that). But deep down, in my heart, I knew it was not just about the money; God wanted all of me and the money could always come later.

CHAPTER 9

THE GREAT DELIVERANCE

It all happened one normal, boring Friday night in this small town, where I had found work to continue my apprenticeship.

It happened while I was standing on the second floor of the apprentice hostel, close to the stairwell, listening to a girl who was singing in the entertainment room on the ground floor.

"Is that a Christian song she's singing?" A voice startled me. Looking up, I noticed this dude with glasses, and he was speaking to me.

"No, I don't think so," I said hastily, hoping he would leave, but no way.

"Are you a Christian?" he continued.

"No, I'm a backslider." I answered almost instinctively, hating myself for saying it, knowing it would provoke this fellow even further into a discussion.

"Would you like to be a Christian again?" he asked eagerly.

"No, I'm not ready for it yet, man," I muttered, and I started moving away from this fellow who was starting to irritate me.

But he moved with me and quickly added, "Please come and join us on Tuesday night. A few of us get together in the apprentice entertainment room to share the good news of Jesus with one another."

"I'll think about it. Thanks," were my departing words to this young messenger of the gospel of Jesus Christ.

The weekend was spent trying to think about something else, except about God and that dude. The face of the man by the stairwell kept coming back to me, and worse were his words, *Are you a Christian?*

My answer, *No, I'm a backslider.* I hardly slept the whole weekend; I desperately needed something or someone.

Tuesday night came, and I was the first one at the apprentice entertainment hall waiting for the church meeting the dude told me about. After a while, a lot of young people started flocking to the hall, some swearing, others smoking. Here was me, unable to understand what kind of church meeting this was going to be. Next thing, a movie projector arrived and was set up, and then a movie started showing. I realised that this was no church meeting. Somewhere, something had gone wrong.

As for me, there was no way I could delay this urge in my spirit any longer, I was now desperately in need of a mighty saviour. Without thinking, I ran out into the hall, up the stairs to my room, and slamming the door behind me, I fell on my knees and wept, like, I really wept, big sobs, begging the Lord for forgiveness of my sins, telling Him how truly sorry I was for my wickedness and all the hurt I had caused Him as my creator and my saviour. I don't know how long I cried and spoke to God, but in the distance, I could hear knocking at the door. I thought at first that I was imagining it. Then it came again and again, very persistently. I didn't want to answer it, as I was busy with very important matters and my eyes were red from the crying. However, the knocking continued. I wanted to shout, "Go away!" but it was persistent. I thought if I waited a while, they would go away, but not a chance.

So, I decided to open the door.

There, in front of me stood a man, clean-shaven, and well dressed in a suit and he immediately greeted me in Afrikaans and said, *"Die Here het my na jou deur gestuur vanaand, ek weet regtig nie hoekom nie."* (God has sent me to your door tonight, and I don't know why).

Shocked, I responded, "Who are you?"

"I'm Dominee (pastor) Vermeulen, from the Afrikaans Baptist Church in town," he responded.

Still trying to digest what just happened, I told him that he would not believe this, but I had just poured out my heart to God and asked Jesus to forgive my sins.

What an obedient child of God this man was! He prayed with me and read from the scripture, encouraging me to stand upon God's Word and trusting that what I desired has, in fact, taken place. I knew with all my heart that something had happened that night that would change my life forever.

The next morning, I reached out for my pipe and tobacco and remembered what had happened, so I immediately put away the pipe, fell on my knees and thanked the Lord Jesus for cleansing me from sin. I also asked Him to give me strength to continue in this newfound way.

I was invited to YFC (Youth for Christ) meetings, which I thoroughly enjoyed and learned once again that I needed to pray, read my Bible daily, and tell others about this wonderful 'Man' Jesus who gave me a new life. Every free opportunity at work (teatime, lunch time, etc.) was spent in prayer and reading my small New Testament Bible.

Telling others about Jesus became so much easier and exciting and since starting a first-year apprenticeship again, I had committed to myself not to tell anyone about my dreadful past, fearing I might lose my job again, and even worse, would be the rejection from normal people.

It was about six months after I started work that I was called into the office by the head of the apprentice training centre.

"Morning, Billy!"

"Please take a seat," he said, pointing to a chair on the other side of the conference table. I noticed quite a few people on his side of the table and wondered what exactly this was all about.

"Billy, when you applied for the apprenticeship, we sent off your documents to the national apprentice board in Johannesburg." *Oh no,* I thought to myself. My heart sunk and I felt lightheaded and kind of knew what was coming next. This scenario had played out so many times since I tried to start my life over again.

"Well, Billy, we were shocked at the report that came back from the board."

I was now looking down, too embarrassed to even lift my head.

"We read all about your drugs, deserting your post, drinking on the job, and gangs."

I could not believe this was happening again.

"But after monitoring your work and work ethics, as well as your relationship with other workers, we made a decision."

Oh no, here comes the bad news, I thought, and I was frantically fidgeting with my fingers, looking on the ground and getting ready to walk out.

"We, as a committee, have decided to give you back the full three-year apprenticeship you had completed at the aircraft company in Johannesburg."

Boom! It hit me between the eyes, I could feel my eyes swelling up, and tears were beginning to run down my cheeks.

"You serious, sir?" I blurted out.

"Absolutely, Billy! We have seen such a change in your life. What happened?"

This was my opportunity to tell them what happened.

"Sir, I met with Jesus in my hostel room one night and at the same time, a local pastor arrived at my door who told me that the Lord had sent him to my room, and I have now committed my life to Jesus and go to church on a regular basis."

The group clapped hands and smiled and shook hands with me.

"Oh, wait a minute, Billy! I nearly forgot.

"We will also be giving you 'back pay' for the six months you worked as a first-year apprentice; you should have been earning more as a third-year apprentice."

Walking back to the workshop, I was now crying and was embarrassed for others to see my red eyes, but these were tears of joy, not sadness. It was the Lord Jesus who once again confirmed that He was now in control of my life, and it was indeed a new start in life for me.

When I received the 'backpay', I was shocked to see that it amounted to almost the exact amount of money I owed people in Johannesburg.

I asked a friend from YFC (Youth for Christ) if he would take me to Johannesburg one weekend to pay the money I owed people. He agreed, and off we went.

The first door I knocked on was that of my uncle, who had lent my dad money to bail me out of prison. His wife (my aunt) opened the door and after hugs and greetings, I handed her the envelope and explained what had happened. She refused to take it, but I pleaded with her, telling her it was the principle of returning to those who had helped me, just as the Lord had ordered me to do. With a lot of tears, she hugged me and accepted.

The next debt was from an old friend whom I knew for many years—we used to take drugs together. His mother opened the door and started crying when I told her who I was (she didn't recognise me). She begged me to stay, as she wanted her son to see what Jesus had done for me. He arrived a while later but showed absolutely no emotion to the change that had taken place in my life. Unfortunately, we also had very little to say to each other.

Photo taken 1976—only six months after my Redemption

This process continued till I handed over the last envelope. It was like I had become a new Billy and a deep peace settled within my spirit.

On the way back to Newcastle, we were singing, rejoicing and praising God in the car for His amazing goodness and love towards us.

One evening, I was invited by a work friend to go with him to the Assemblies of God church in town. I agreed and really enjoyed the meeting. The people were also so friendly, even though they didn't know me. I started attending all their meetings on a regular basis and knew that God wanted us (his children) to have a regular place of worship and that He would place us in the fellowship where He could use us, as the Bible says:

> *For the Lord has placed you in the body as it has pleased Him (1 Corinthians 12:18).*

I remained in that same little church for thirteen years (by the grace of God). I have always believed that whatever you do, you must do it well or don't do it at all. (A principle my father constantly reminded me of).

I got involved with a singing group in the Assemblies of God church I was attending. Here, we are singing an item at an Easter Convention in a large tent. (I am in the white shirt) from a very young age I enjoyed singing, mostly with my brothers and also with my dearest mom.

When I was a gang member, I was a 'staunch' member, come wind, hail, rain or snow. I never missed a gang meeting.

The principle applies more so to Christians because we deal with eternal matters; we can't afford to be lukewarm or half-hearted; it is either hot or cold, everything or nothing.

If you are neither hot nor cold, I will spew you out of My mouth (Revelation 3:16).

Weather and feelings should never influence my fervour for serving God.

As a young man, I realised that I needed a lovely Christian girl to share my life with. There were a lot of young girls in the church I was now attending, but I was looking for someone special.

Having been involved with girls from a young age, I knew the qualities I was looking for at this point in my life—much of what I had not really seen in girls who didn't know our Lord Jesus. It was indeed a tall order, but I had seen too many things in my life to settle for less.

One night, a lady in the church came to me and said, "Billy, I had a dream last night. It was about you, walking down the aisle of the church with a young girl."

I laughed out loud.

"And where might this young lady be?" I asked. "And who might she be?" I added.

"Well, unfortunately, she used to be in the church, but her parents moved away, but I believe they will be returning to Newcastle some time."

"Mmmm, okay. Noted," I said, a little disappointed that she was not there.

Having forgotten all about our talk, some two weeks later, I met this 'mysterious girl' at a youth meeting and barbeque at one of the elders' homes. There was an introduction, and after a few visits to her house, I really liked her, only to discover she was only fifteen years old. I tried to put off seeing her again, but love is too strong and our great God had a hand in this meeting for sure.

When I told my father I was seeing a girl of fifteen years old, he obviously thought the worst and told me to think seriously about things. He even contacted her parents to warn them about me. But fortunately, God had planned it all, and two years later we walked down the aisle, just as that lady in the church had dreamed.

The wedding day was so different; my wife's parents hired the townhall and we invited family from both sides and our entire congregation from the church where we were in fellowship. We had about 250 people at the wedding, sang choruses and had a feast for a king. One of the special guests was the lady who had a dream about me and this young girl walking down the aisle.

The joke of the day at the wedding and still a joke in our family to this day is that I had booked the first night in a lovely guest house halfway to our honeymoon destination, which was to be a hotel in the Drakensberg Mountains. However, the guest house was named Fort Mistake Guest House. It was, in fact, named after an old British fort, that was built during the Boer War.

*On our wedding day. I was 24 and Aileen
my wife was 17 yrs.*

It was a glorious day and God had given me my heart's desire. The verse in the Bible that has become so much a part of my life is:

> *Delight thyself also in the Lord and He will give
> you the desires of your heart. Commit your way
> unto the Lord trust also in Him and He will
> bring it to pass (Psalm 37: 4-5).*

We have now been happily married for 46 years, and both know without a doubt that marriage is of God and requires contributions from both husband and wife. What you put in, you both get out. Both husband and wife must work at their relationship, first with God, then towards each other, and finally towards their children.

We have three beautiful children, a son and two daughters and each of them is married to a wonderful partner. In total, my wife and I boast of our 12 beautiful grandchildren.

My son heard me give my testimony many times, even out there in the wilderness areas of Botswana to the San people with an interpreter, and when I share about my late mother and how I should have told her more often how much I love her while she was still alive, he begins to cry and tells me afterwards that he does love me and he's so glad I'm not a 'rebel, drug addict and fighter' anymore, and that I now love and serve our Lord Jesus.

CHAPTER 10

RISE UP AND WALK

Jesus found me in my derelict state, through a simple word spoken by a stranger inviting me to a church meeting, and then, alone in a hostel room, crying unto God for mercy. The Lord sends an obedient child of his to knock on my door to confirm that my cry has been heard in the very heavens.

Indeed, this miraculous redemption is one of the most amazing experiences (both physical and spiritual) I have ever had and probably will have on this earth.

The result of this incredible encounter with Jesus set my life on a truly heaven-bound road—not a road of constant rebellion and deception, but rather one of absolute truth and real life. A road that would take me well into the future, to be exact, some 49 years (now as I am typing). Thank you, Jesus, for finding me in my pitiful state and even stooping down to lift me out of the deep mire and sin of this world.

Many have asked me to share more of what has happened in my life after such a great salvation. So, of course, 49 years is a long time and would probably take quite a few books to cover it all. However, after much prayer and consideration, I believe it is important to just touch on certain important aspects of my life that have taken place over these many years, especially to dispel any thoughts that it has been smooth sailing with only great blessings along the way.

Great blessings indeed have been bountiful, but so has much suffering, heartache, and difficult times. Yet through it all, I can truly say that Jesus has never left my side; in fact without Him by my side, I almost definitely would never have made it thus far.

I'll take you back to the small town of Newcastle in South Africa, where the Lord brought about my miraculous salvation.

I met Aileen, my dearest wife, when she was 15 and I was 22. We got engaged when she was 16 and married when she was 17, and our first child (a son) was born when Aileen was 18.

It was as if I was already in heaven with my son's birth, from wallowing in the deep mire of sin, unable to escape the chains of addiction, hate, aggression, and hopelessness, to now having a beautiful wife and my very own son, my firstborn. How unbelievable and miraculous is that? We went on to be blessed with two more beautiful children, both girls, and our family was then complete.

While working for a large corporate steel manufacturer in Newcastle for many years, I completed my trade apprenticeship as a fitter and turner and was now fully qualified with many responsibilities at work. I had a young Zulu man as my assistant, whom I was training. He also took great care of the equipment we serviced daily. He could not, however, speak English and I could not speak Zulu, so it was indeed a challenge for both of us, but I believe that the Lord had purposed it so.

I would read my small New Testament Bible during tea and lunch breaks every day, and the word soon spread that I was a child of God. This young man taught me very basic Zulu, and I taught him very basic English. Once I had left the corporation many years later, I heard that he had done a ministerial course and was considering going into full-time work as a minister. I look forward to meeting him in heaven one day, as we have so much to talk about.

Just another normal working day and I was summoned to report to the office of the head of maintenance division.

"Morning Billy! Any idea why we have called you into the office this morning," the head of the maintenance department asked me, waiting for an answer.

"No sir! Maybe something has gone wrong at the site I must attend to urgently?"

"No, it's to do with a promotion; we would like you to consider taking up the senior planner post in the

current maintenance division you report to."

Well, I certainly did not need any time to consider this offer. I was now married, had a child and had been praying that the Lord would open doors for extra income.

Much to their surprise I answered:

"Sir, I really don't need to consider it at all. It's a definite *yes* from me. When would you like me to start?"

"Good. Your training will start next week," the head of division answered and congratulated me.

I remember crying as I drove home that day with such a grateful heart for our Lord for His great provision. This was to be the first of a few promotions within the same corporate company since my salvation.

No way am I suggesting that when you get saved, you get promotions, but what I do believe is that my heart was fully dedicated firstly to the Lord and when I went to work each day, I worked hard with all my attention on the job and was always willing to go the extra mile. I showed the love of Christ to all, no matter their ethnic background. My desire was and still is to please God in all that I do.

Please understand that I was not perfect. I was still struggling with many things from my past, but as Paul says in the Bible in:

> *Philippians 3:14: I press on toward the mark for the prize of the high calling of God in Christ Jesus.*

While working hard, I did not want to be consumed by the secular world, as I was also busy settling into a church, where I believed (and still do) that we must be an integral part of a fellowship where we can be ministered to and minister to others. The Bible says in:

> *1 Corinthians 12:18: But now hath God set the members every one of them in the body of Christ (the church), as it hath pleased Him.*

After my redemption, the Lord steered me in the direction of a small local church in this small town, some 300km east of Johannesburg. I was blown away by the absolute truth that was ministered from the pulpit. It was not always promised blessings, but it was the unadulterated word of God that, at many times, cut deep into the heart. In fact, it was exactly what I needed at this point in my life. Having come out of a deep mire, there has to be no compromise. You must commit fully, just as you committed to your own evil desires; you must commit to that level, plus even more, to ensure a good and close walk with God.

One Sunday morning, arriving early at church, I was approached by one of the church elders.

"Morning, Billy! Would you like to stand by the door and welcome the people as they enter the church? A handshake and hand them a hymn and chorus book."

"Absolutely," I answered without hesitation.

In the moment, I was taken back a little, as my personality was still very much one of being 'aloof' caused by the drugs I had used for so many years and having avoided normal people during that time, as well as my lack of interaction with them as well as my English language, which had deteriorated so badly due to only speaking 'slang' for so many years.

But this was the beginning of a healing process for my relationship with people and my speech and language.

Ironically, many years later, I bought and owned an English language school that was part of an international franchise, specialising in teaching English to foreigners. It became a family joke—can you believe it? Billy owning an English language school. Ha! Ha! It is so good that one can laugh about these things once you have been brought through them; however, it does not diminish in any way my great appreciation to our Lord Jesus for His transforming power.

I would put everything into the meet and greet at the church door, and when the people left the church, I'd take back the hymn and chorus books and wish them well, which became truly fulfilling. Once they had left, I would clean up the church and leave as well. This was super gratifying to my soul in that I could offer this humble service to the Lord for all His great goodness towards me. I was not doing it to earn his blessing; I was doing this because of His great love towards me, which is so difficult for me to comprehend.

Eventually, I was opening and locking up the church on a regular basis. The Lord had kept His mighty hand upon me, and the time eventually came when I was officially appointed as a serving deacon in the church.

Another passion I developed was working with youth in the church. We started a youth group on Friday nights, which we called, 'winners'.

We decided the best way to get the young people to the church was to collect and drop them off. The church owned a VW Kombi, and one of the members of the church who owned a garage also had a Kombi. So, the youth service began for young people aged 12 to 16 years, and eventually we added a second meeting we called, 'senior youth' targeting older youth.

The Lord added many young people to the church. In fact, on a Friday night, we could get up to 40 young people at our early 'winners' meeting and some 25 at the later 'senior youth' meeting.

The Lord was working mightily in this little town of Newcastle in Kwa Zulu Natal, and I was so excited to be a small part of the mighty work He was doing.

"Morning, Billy."

The foreman looked at me across the room where the maintenance team were sitting and standing in his office for the normal early morning meeting, and as maintenance planner, I was now handing out the maintenance tasks that needed to be done on the plant for the day.

"Morning, Boss," I responded.

"There has been a request for you to head up to the main admin office outside the plant for an interview this morning," the foreman said with a smile on his face. Everyone in the office turned to look at me and I felt a little awkward.

"What's this all about, Billy?" The group wanted to know from me when all I could do was shrug my shoulders.

"I seriously don't know anything about it, guys." Not wanting to attract more attention to myself.

But this was indeed to be another step up in the corporation for me. The Lord's hand was on the interview, and by the end of that month, I was in a fancy office on the 3rd floor wearing a long sleeve smart shirt and tie. I was in the 'Glass House', as we used to call it.

The promotion this time was, in fact, to move into a senior maintenance planner position, where I would be part of a team of five people teaching maintenance planners throughout the factory all about computer-generated maintenance tasks.

Once again, I rejoiced in the goodness of God and His great provision towards me, who was indeed a 'rubbish' in the eyes of many, including my own, but now I was a child of the living God, washed in the blood of Jesus, and saved by His mighty hand. A new life indeed!

The glass house (ISCOR Admin block). My 2nd promotion at the factory in Newcastle.

While at the church I was attending, we had gone through the foundational teachings, and I was given quite a few opportunities to preach on Sunday nights.

From a very young age, I enjoyed singing, and even in my real bad days, I would end up singing one of the Beetles old songs, i.e. *Rocky Raccoon,* in the pub to get a few complimentary drinks.

The Lord had opened miraculous doors for us to purchase our first house, a wonderful place where we could raise our children and settle down.

It was way more house than what we expected and needed, but certainly our very own. It allowed me to get involved in doing home and garden refurbishment, which I had no idea that I could do, but nevertheless I attempted tiling, building retainer walls and so much more. The truth is, I surprised myself and thanked the Lord for giving me such hope, which never existed before I had met Him.

We had settled into the community in the small town of Newcastle, Kwa Zulu Natal, South Africa. However, things were not going well in South Africa at that stage due to the government policies of the day.

I decided to voluntarily join the local military commando unit to ensure I did my part in protecting the community and my family where the Lord had placed us and where we had now settled down.

Once again, I committed myself to whatever I was going to do, but I always attempted not to let those things affect my place in my growing family and, even more importantly, my place in the local church where the Lord had placed me.

Soviet SPM Limpet mine attacks were becoming the order of the day in the town where we were staying, while the murder rate was increasing almost daily in and around the rural areas of the town.

Within a short time after completing specific commando training, I was appointed as lance corporal and then full corporal. A specialised reaction force unit was established to counteract the onslaught of the terrorist attacks on industry, local communities, together with public and government facilities. Special urban warfare training camps were arranged for the unit, along with advanced military driving skills, etc.

A few photos from my time in the commandos.

Having obtained top marks during these camps, I was soon promoted to reaction force platoon sergeant. Much different from my naval training in Simonstown, where my life was probably at its lowest ebb, filled with drugs, drink, despair, and gloom, I was now disciplined, excited and proud of what I had become, i.e. a child of God.

The year was 1987, and my oldest son had started school while my wife and I were also very involved in church life, and I can really say we were content.

On the work front, I was requested to apply for a position at the company's head office in Pretoria. They were urgently looking for a team of six specialists to start up a major project that would see the development and implementation of computerised maintenance systems throughout all its factories and plants both in South Africa and Namibia.

After much prayer, I decided to apply, as it not only meant a promotion but also an increase in salary, and more importantly, I felt the stirring of the Spirit of God in my heart. My cosy nest was about to be ruffled again. Not too long after my application was submitted, I had a phone call from head office asking me to get to Pretoria for an interview.

The Lord had just opened another door, and within a few months we were in Pretoria, the Lord had blessed us so much that we were able to purchase a new house and I settled into my new position quite easily. The specialised project team was given a target date of three years in which to install this huge maintenance system that ran on personal computers (PCs) and not mainframe computers. PCs had just broken into the market, so we were immersed in extensive computer training as well as installation and design of local area networks.

The project lasted the full three years, and, in that time, we were blessed to be part of a wonderful local church in the area. The ministry I was blessed with grew to the point of allowing me to take Bible studies as well as preach the gospel quite extensively in the region. My wife and I felt a special connection with the believers in the church and really thought this was to be our home until retirement.

However, our journey was far from over; the best was yet to come, and so was the ruffling of our nest. Just when I feel that this is it, time to settle, it's as if the Lord says, *No Billy, there is still way too much to do.* Before we know it, we are moving again, to the dismay of family and friends who could not understand why.

Strange I could scarcely understand it. How on earth was I going to try explaining this to others?

CHAPTER 11

PROSPER AND TESTING TIMES

The maintenance project at head office had lasted three years and was now coming to an end. The implementation was very successful and done within budget. I was now 37 years old and could not believe how quick these three years had gone.

Because of the project's success, the head office offered each one of the six members of the project team the opportunity to manage the implementation and training of the software in different factories around the country and abroad in Namibia.

While considering these options, I was approached by the computer company that had won the tender to supply all the equipment for the project (worth millions) and asked if I would be at all interested in joining their company and assisting the manager of a new branch office they had recently opened in Durban on the East Coast of South Africa.

I was now 37 and had a strong urge to achieve my goals and care for my family. After a few days of fasting and prayer, I accepted their offer and not many weeks later, myself, my dearest wife, our children, and Muggsy, my American Pitbull dog, were on our way to stay in Durban.

The church in Durban heard we were making our way down to the coast and asked if we would like to stay in the old church manse, which had just been refurbished and perhaps assist the local pastor wherever and whenever possible. We agreed, and on our arrival in Durban the very next day, our furniture arrived, and we moved into the house next to the church.

Then something strange happened that almost sent us packing back to Pretoria. However, in hindsight and after some counselling, we realised it was a direct attack of the Devil on our lives.

Once we had moved all the furniture into the house, I started installing the curtains throughout the house.

While I was busy in the main lounge area, there was a knock at the door. I went to open the door straight away, thinking perhaps it was one of the church people or the pastor coming to welcome us to the house and church, which was right next door.

As I opened the door, I was greeted by a youngish man with very short hair who was approximately six feet tall and very sun-scorched. He said he desperately needed a bath, and could I assist.

Well, to be honest, I was new to this 'pastor's house' thing and said he must rather go see if there is someone by the church who can assist him, and off he went, not a word of thanks, only a blank stare.

I continued with the curtains, only to be disturbed again by a knock a few minutes later.

On opening the door, the same young man stood by the door and said, "The young people at the church said I must ask you for a shower." That was it—no emotion, no please, just a blank stare.

I should have seen the writing on the wall, but wanting to help my fellow man, I asked him to take a seat in the lounge where I was busy working, while I asked my wife to run a bath.

My young daughter and son were sitting in the lounge and watching this dude. He was saying nothing, so I tried to start some kind of conversation.

"So, where are you from?" I asked.

"Here," was his blunt answer.

Then he stood up and walked to the centre of the lounge, where my wife had set out the glass coffee table with a lovely big vase. He picked up the vase and started admiring it. I was busy threading stretch cord through a lace curtain and asked him if he liked the vase.

He looked me straight in the eyes with that blank stare, did a 360-degree turn, and threw the vase at a beautiful big wall-mounted mirror I had just hung up above the fireplace with all his might.

The vase smashed into hundreds of pieces, together with the mirror that was now smashed to smithereens. The kids ran screaming out of the lounge and I jumped up to face this threat head-on, almost feeling the old Billy suddenly being awakened, while at the same time shouting to my wife to bring my pistol. We had a special name for the gun so that it would not frighten the kids when we spoke about it.

My wife came running out of the room and into the lounge, while I was busy with a close face-to-face standoff with this dude much taller than me and me trying to pre-empt his next move. She slipped me the gun, and I took a step back, cocked the gun, pointed it straight at his head and told him to get out of my house.

Unbelievably, he did not flinch or move towards the door.

I started shouting at the top of my voice, "Get out my house or I will blow your brains all over this new carpet!" But not a flinch from him.

While this was happening, I heard my American Pitbull (Muggsy) going mad at the back door. It was a deep, angry, consistent growl, and plenty of scratching on the door.

I shouted to my wife, "Aileen, let Muggsy in!"

She ran to the door and flung it open.

I could now hear Muggsy's growl getting louder and his paws slipping on the kitchen floor as he speedily headed to the main lounge without any coaxing from my wife or myself.

I looked at Muggsy as he entered the lounge. It was as if his eyes connected with mine; I glanced at this dude and I noticed the dude's eyes were big and filled with some kind of fear. I looked back at my dog, and his mouth was frothing, his head down, mouth open. I knew instinctively that he was coming in for the kill.

The dude was now doing another 360-degree spin, but this time trying to aim for the door. After almost missing a stride, he reached the door. I lashed out with my foot and kicked him in the back to assist him on his way out. He fell out of the doorway, and as he stood up, Muggsy was now on top of him and had bitten into the back of his neck and wouldn't let go. He started to run down the long driveway with Muggsy still on his back and his teeth clenched. His arms were frantically trying to hit Muggsy but were unable to reach him.

They disappeared down the road. I checked on my family and made sure they were all okay. I took my gun and ran down the driveway in hot pursuit, but as I got to the main road, all I could see in the distance was Muggsy strolling home, mouth full of blood and looking very satisfied.

I couldn't see the dude anywhere. I checked my dog over to make sure he was not hurt, but all looked good, so I patted and embraced him.

"Good boy, good boy Muggsy!" I said over and over.

When I returned home, my wife and kids were in tears, and they wanted to return to Pretoria immediately.

These regular moves were indeed taking their toll on not only my family but, in a way, also on me. Just as the kids make new friends at school, it's time to move. We get settled into a church and make some wonderful friends and then we go off again.

In hindsight, it's easy to look back and see how the Lord was working in all our lives, but when one is going through the actual move – selling homes, changing jobs, churches, and friends – it is very difficult to comprehend how it will all turn out and if each one in the family can survive another move.

Now we had to face this traumatic welcome to our latest home and city.

As a family, we sat down and discussed this satanic attack on our family and home and believed we must continue to wait on God for His wisdom and guidance. We did struggle to sleep for quite a few nights, but as the days went by and the more we spoke about this intrusion, there was a realisation that this was indeed the work of the Devil and that the Lord must surely have a great work for us to do here in this corner of His vineyard, if this is the kind of welcome we got into our new city.

We did contact the police and never heard or saw this dude again. It sounded like he may have been an escaped convict or on parole (according to the police).

I was extremely glad I did not have to shoot the dude; can you imagine the scenario at our first Sunday morning at the church meeting?

'We want to welcome our new assistant pastor Billy, and his family, who unfortunately had to kill someone in self-defence on his first day moving into the church manse'.

Praise the Lord, this was not to be, and all ended well, and we settled in with no one in the church even aware of what had taken place.

CHAPTER 12

GROWTH AND PAINFUL MOMENTS

One of the pastors in our church had spent many years involved in mission work with the San People in Botswana, and, in fact, to this day (as I write), he is still faithfully ministering to the San people and establishing small churches for these wonderful people throughout the country of Botswana.

My son was now around 12 and I was 38, and I had arranged to take a group of young men and boys from the local church to do a mission trip with this pastor in the outback areas of Botswana to the San people.

It was to be the beginning of many trips into Botswana, in fact, mostly with young people from all around the world on missions, safaris and doing community work.

One day, I heard about a businessman (who was also a lay preacher) who would be sharing with the local community 'how to start your own business', at a high school that my kids were attending. He was a very successful businessman who had started up some big franchises in South Africa and internationally. At this point in my life, I had a desire (which I believe God had put in my heart) to continue to work with young people. Having two teenagers of my own, I wanted to somehow ensure that young people knew about another way to enjoy life and appreciate this beautiful country that we live in, i.e. South Africa.

So, I decided to attend the four information sessions that were to be held at the high school hall every Thursday evening.

I certainly was not a businessman, but I had a God-given vision (I believe) and desire for the youth of the world.

The sessions were extremely informative, and the vision began to grow in my heart and spirit. So, after the last session, I remember going up to the businessman and asking him if it was possible to see him privately at his office in connection with starting a business. He agreed to give me 30 minutes of his time. At the meeting, I will never forget his words to me.

"Billy, make a list of all the things you're very good at doing, but be exceptionally honest with yourself," he said. "Then make a list of all the things you absolutely love doing and see if there are any two items on those lists that link up; if so, that is probably a good place to start your research, and move in that direction, waiting on God, most importantly," he added.

Well, my lists were not that long, but there were indeed two items that linked up on paper and within my heart and spirit.

I am very good at organising, if left to do it myself (honestly).

I love the outdoors, wildlife, Africa and young people.

So these items were linked on paper, and the research began. Not long after that, *Youth Adventures* was born and continued for 14 years, eventually growing into a company that employed some 39 staff in two countries in sub-Saharan Africa and eventually forming part of a group of three companies that I owned with approximately 40,000 people (mostly youth from around the world), utilising our services over the 14 years we were in operation. We also indirectly financially supported no less than 19 wildlife conservation companies throughout Africa.

My wife, oldest daughter, and I were the first three employees, working temporarily during the school holidays while I still held an IT job. We pioneered taking up to 50 students in busses camping in sub-Saharan Africa. The groups were made up of schools, universities, and church youth groups. This was indeed what I dreamed about, and now it was happening. The first three years, my daughter, wife and I did it all with these large groups from marketing, camping, food preparation, guiding, bookings, activities, etc. Most of the groups in the first three years were locals from South Africa.

Then the opportunity arose for me to market abroad and to attend international travel shows. This was intimidating, as I had never been overseas (out of Africa). Once we entered the international market, things took off, and bookings started to flood in.

We could no longer work from my dining room at home, so we moved into offices just 10 minutes' ride from the house (*our first business move*).

The Lord's hand of blessing was upon us as a family as well as business; I had absolutely no doubt about that; however, more of my time was being spent on tour with the student groups, while at the same time training up new guides on how to cross borders with our large groups and taking good care of the clientele.

The business continued to grow, and the offices need to be upgraded to bigger premises once again (*our second business move*).

This time we added in a 129-bed backpacker lodge in Durban main town with an international language school and the safari tour operation all under one roof.

The team and our company vehicles at the first office block close to our house.

Our four-star backpacker lodge had 129 beds, a pool, restaurant, an internet café, language school, and travel company.

Our last move as a company was to this lovely office block in a stunning area in Durban.

While still enjoying the untold blessings of the Lord on our lives and business, we now had to separate the language school and the group's main head office to new premises in the upmarket area of Umhlanga Rocks (*our third and final move*).

As one can imagine, we were going from strength to strength and the Lord had blessed me with new innovative ideas for the youth travel industry. These ideas I introduced only to see a few years later (and even today as I write) that one of the innovative ideas I developed and introduced into the market had gone on to be one of the fastest growing sectors in the world travel industry and is now said to be worth an estimated 2 billion USD.

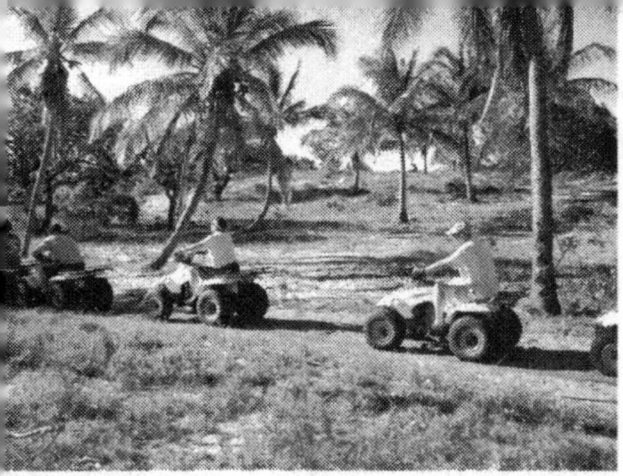
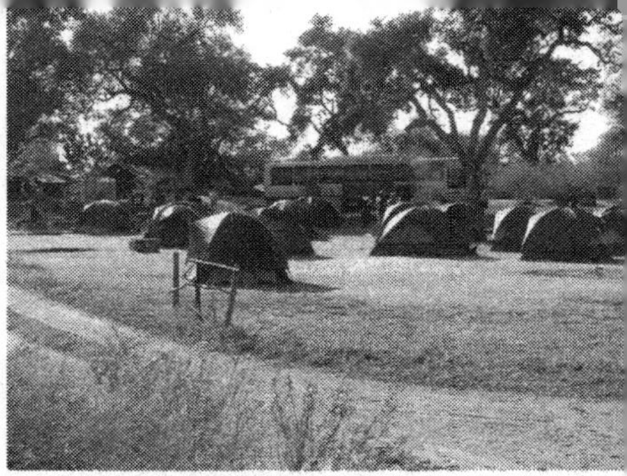
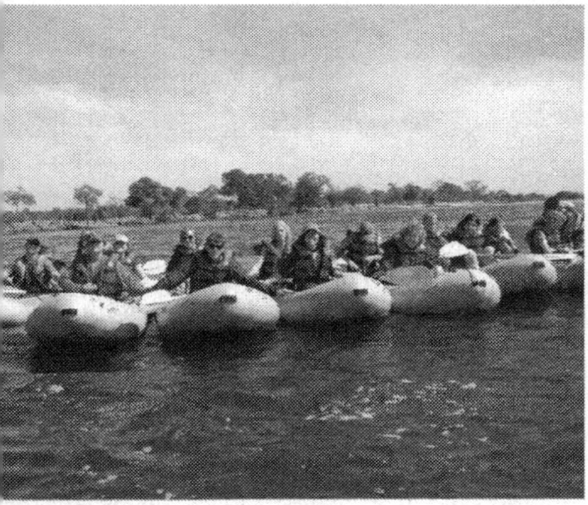
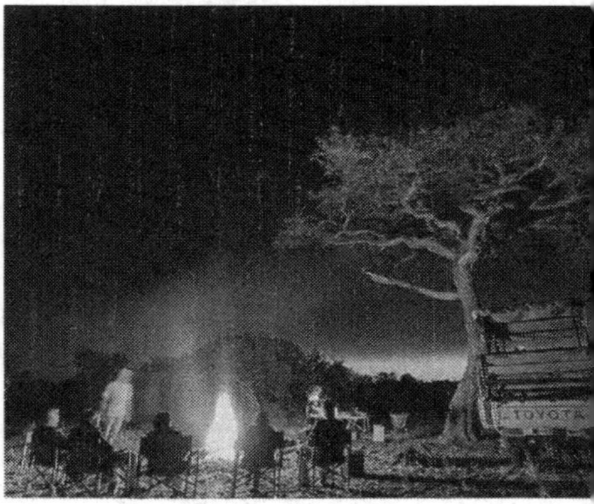
TOYOTA
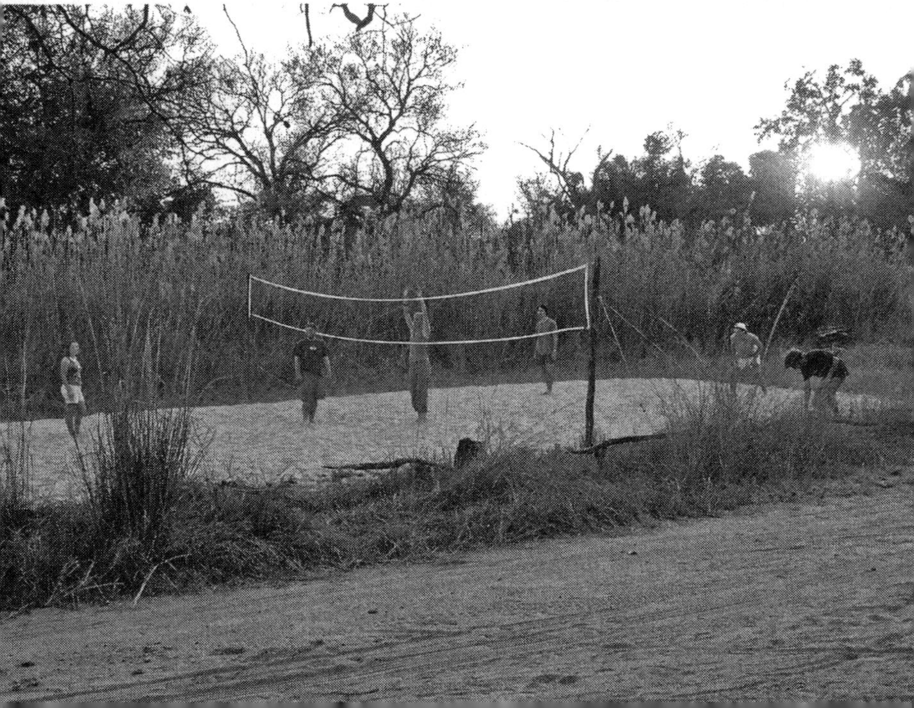

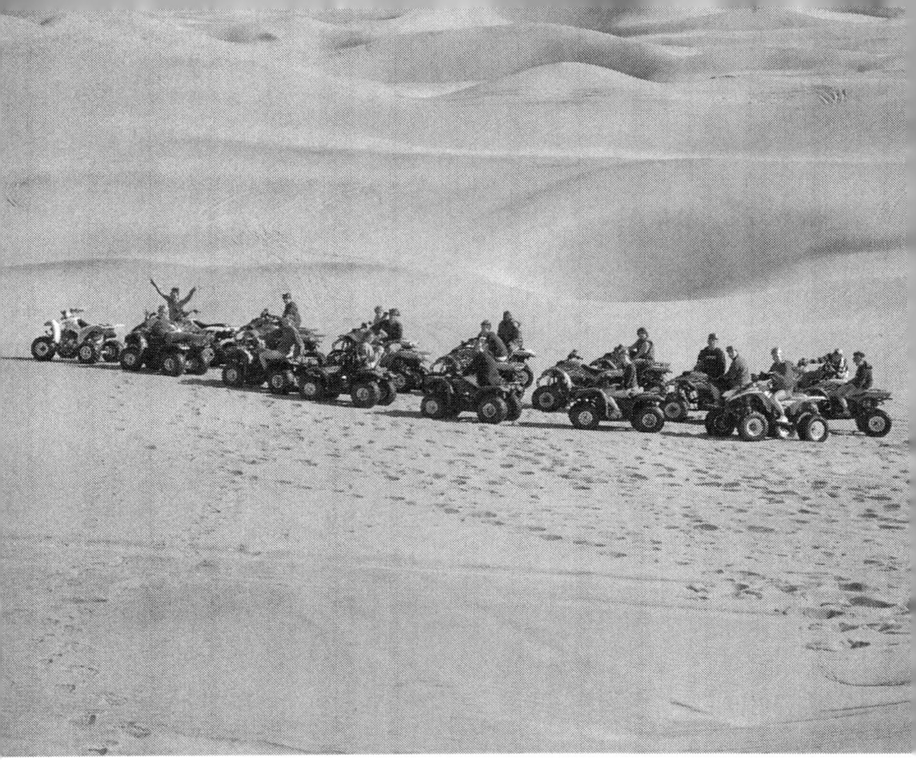

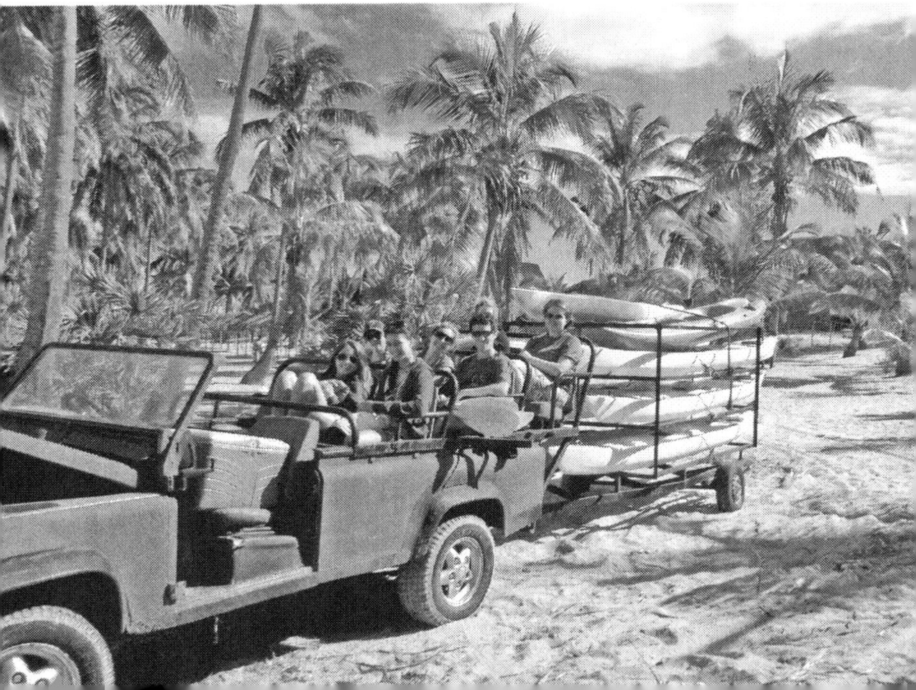

The photos above will give you a little insight into my daily life since starting my youth safari adventure business. Fulfilling my passion for youth, adventure, and love for Africa.

I was blessed to visit 31 countries around the world while in business, mostly for marketing and exhibiting at tourism travel shows as well as doing mission outreach programmes.

The Lord had blessed our business so much, and I wanted to be able to give back wherever possible.

One morning, while checking my email, I noticed an email from a pastor from Asia. The email was a request to find out if I would be willing to come and share my testimony in the Philippine Islands, as there had been some serious things happening with some of the young people in his church.

I sat and looked at this email almost in unbelief, thinking to myself, *Where on earth are the Philippine Islands?* I had absolutely no idea but felt a tugging in my spirit to respond anyway, which I did, saying it would be a pleasure and an honour.

I remember getting up from my office table and saying to my wife, "Honey, I have just agreed to share my testimony in the Philippine Islands."

"You what?" came the answer.

"Do you have any idea where that is, Billy?"

"Umm! No, do you?" I asked.

"No," she answered.

"Okay, well, I'm soon going to find out," I responded, almost sarcastically.

Well, not even two months later, I was in the Philippine Islands with a Christian pop group from South Africa that I had invited to join me. This was to be the beginning of many mission trips to the Philippine Islands to share music and gospel.

A wonderful time of ministry in the Philippines.

South African Christian pop group performing in the Philippine Islands

South African Christian rap group in the Philippines.

South African Christian rock band in the Philippines.

Brazil outreach with my Portuguese interpreter also 'note the pulpit'.

One of the many schools where I shared my testimony.

Above are photos of just a few of the many doors the Lord had opened for me to share my story of His incredible power to save from the gutter most to the uttermost.

What a blessing this was to me, each of us who participated and all those wonderful children of God around Africa and different parts of the world I had the opportunity to visit and meet with. I look forward to the day we meet in heaven, and we can rejoice and worship our Lord Jesus together, never to be apart again.

It was such a blessing, while in a good financial position, to be able to sponsor Christian musical groups from South Africa to accompany me on these many outreaches abroad and throughout Southern Africa. I will forever be grateful to these young people for their absolute willingness, without any hesitation, to join me as we shared the gospel abroad.

Above all, I want to thank our Lord Jesus for the way in which He used me. Someone who was indeed previously vile and evil, now washed in the blood of Jesus and able to share His absolute greatness, mercy and love with others. What an honour and privilege that will be remembered by me forever.

The Lord had opened so many doors to share the great redemption work He had done in my life; however, one of the most interesting places where I shared my testimony was at the same little church that my parents went to for many years. It was also the very same church where the pastor prayed for me at the age of 11, and I was healed of rheumatic fever. I will never forget. During the service, I thanked all the ladies who had prayed with my dearest mom for so many years for the salvation of me and my brothers. I was happy to tell them that the Lord had answered their prayers, and I was living proof of that, even though my dearest mother was not able to enjoy the moment.

After the service, as I greeted the people at the door, a little old lady came up to me and showed me a small black book that looked extremely withered and worn. She turned to a page and pointed. With tears in my eyes, I saw my name as well as my brothers: 'Billy, Johnny and Danny Fourie desperately need salvation'.

"Billy, I think we will now remove your name from our prayer book and note that our prayers have been answered," she said, smiling. "It's been on our list for almost ten years."

Wiping the tears from my eyes now, and a little embarrassed, I answered her, "Aunty, please could you keep our names on that list, but not for salvation as this has been answered 100%, but please pray that our Lord Jesus will keep us three boys till we all meet in the portals of heaven one day."

My mother was indeed a prayer warrior and would never give up, no matter what. It was indeed her prayers and those of her friends in church, as well as those of my loving sister and my dearest dad that brought me out of the deepest, darkest dungeon of sin and despair and translated me into the beautiful brightness of His glorious kingdom.

It was 2009, and back at home in South Africa, there was great excitement in the industry for the upcoming FIFA World Cup (football) to be held in South Africa for the first time in 2010. Word spread in every sector of the South African economy. Planning for this event for most tourism businesses started in early 2009. Our company had great ideas and action plans were put into place for this great event that was to be held in our country.

However, as the months went by, news from my different agents around the world was not good, in that flights were booking up early and this was going to have a devastating effect on my normal large groups of students. Sunshine was replaced with dark clouds of doom and despair. The closer we got to the end of 2009, the worse things got as many of my travel groups had by now cancelled their bookings for the 2010 summer holidays, mostly due to 'lack of flight availability' as well as a concern for the safety of the student groups.

December 2009 was approaching, and I had a sick feeling that we might be in serious trouble with the business. The banks were not at all interested in 'bridging finance' due to the enormous bank collapse in the USA in 2008 and only started affecting South Africa around 2009.

I was now in a serious time of fasting and prayer, begging the Lord Jesus to help me through this mighty storm that was approaching that would decimate not only my business but would have a devastating effect on my family, our staff and business colleagues, both local and abroad. It was as though there was absolutely no response from heaven. I had very little time to make some very big decisions, and I just felt so helpless.

I cried many nights and days trying to understand how this could be happening to me.

Some tough decisions had to be made, i.e. cut staff, cut overheads, and see if we could ride the storm. Sadly, it was not to be, the storm peaked in May 2010, and we lost everything—*yes, I mean everything!* The business, vehicles, our home, friends, business colleagues and so much more. You instantly become hated by everyone (or so it feels), and each person has their own idea (to this day) as to how you came to your demise. However, the Lord knows the details, and He alone is the one who really cares during these tough and terrible times.

All I could do was hang on to Jesus with all my heart. He had brought me out of such despair and mire. *Surely this is nothing for Him to make right,* I thought.

I feared the phone and slept a lot to try and deaden the reality of what was happening to me. I could not face people at church any longer; there were just too many questions I had to try and answer, and the wounds were deep. We, as a family, were hurting badly. So, I stayed away from church as well; probably not the wisest decision, but it was exactly how I felt at that time, forsaken, depressed, forgotten, and cast aside.

It took me weeks, if not months, to recover and not without tremendous guilt, hurt and pain. Also for those the demise of my business affected locally and across the world.

After many weeks of tears and sorrow, I slowly started to get back to fellowship so that the goodness of our Lord

Jesus could fill my now totally empty soul and totally downcast spirit.

One day, I met up with a young businessman in the new church we started attending who had also recently lost his IT business. In fact, his business went down just a few months before I lost mine. He and I were able to comfort and uplift one another in the Lord whenever the opportunity arose. I am not even sure till this day that he will know what an effect his encouragement had upon my life during that 'oh so difficult time'.

I could slowly feel the goodness of the Lord begin to flood my soul again, filling me with a little hope, a little love and a little peace over time. I was now more open to my daily reminder by the Holy Spirit of the great and miraculous intervention that brought me out of deep darkness and translated me into His great and marvellous light on my day of salvation in that small hostel room in a small town of Newcastle in South Africa and so what had happened to my business was absolutely nothing in comparison to His mighty power to do what He knows is best for me and the family.

In hindsight, I do believe that the Lord was answering my prayers, but not the way I had hoped, but then again, He is the Lord Almighty and knows all things. This part of my life since my salvation was, indeed, both a time of great blessing and also a very trying time for me and my family, as well as the many staff I had employed. It was indeed the closest I had come to just throwing in the towel on everything. *But God!*

I was so reminded when Jesus told Peter just before He was about to be crucified that Satan had desired to have him that he might sift him as wheat.

> *But Jesus said to Peter, I have prayed for you Peter that your Faith may not fail. And when you have turned back strengthen your brethren (Luke 22:31).*

Was this indeed my testing time to see what meant more to me—the Giver of Life or what life can give me?

It had now come to the point where I desperately needed to earn an income to continue to sustain my dearest wife, myself, and my youngest daughter.

My older son and daughter were married and had their own families, jobs, and things to take care of.

"Lord Jesus, please, can you give me wisdom and open a door that would be best for my family and I?" This was a daily prayer and cry from my heart to our wonderful Lord and saviour.

We now had to vacate the apartment we had owned and had lost and were concerned as to 'what now'? The answer came 'just in time' with only one door opening, and it was kind of weird as it meant we needed to move to Italy.

Something we never would have dreamed of doing, once again, *but God!* It was three to four months after the business officially closed that we were on our way to Italy, scared and feeling totally out of control, not really knowing what plans God had for us in a strange country, strange language with very little to our name. The one great positive is that my son and his dearest wife had invited us to come stay with them in an apartment in Milan.

We seriously had no idea what to expect in a strange country, but we had, by the grace of God, reached a point where we knew that God was in control. Not an easy lesson to learn at all, yet vital when faced with such distress and hopelessness.

CHAPTER 13

TIME OF RESTORATION

"Morning, dear," I said to my wife early one morning, as I could hear the traffic begin below in the streets of Milan.

"Morning, Billy," came the reply.

"It's time to start teaching English, here in Milan," I blurted out before saying anything else.

"Are you sure?" she asked.

"Without a doubt, I have to at least try," I said, without any hesitation.

Having owned an English language school in South Africa, I also completed a TEFL course (Teaching English as a Foreign Language) before departing for Italy. I was ready to give it a good go.

I advertised in a local monthly English tabloid in Milan, offering English language courses in the evening at a private college.

The response was indeed phenomenal. With my first class starting, I needed to get two additional teachers to assist me, and we had three levels, so three classes with a minimum of 15 students in each class. Hallelujah! Thank you, Jesus!

A couple who responded to my advert for English teachers were missionaries from the USA who were English teachers and desperately needed the extra income to see them through each month. I had no doubt at all that this was indeed the Lord's doing.

We slowly settled down in Italy with a two-year work visa and eventually moved to a small village on Lake Como. Still trying to understand exactly what the Lord wanted for us in this corner of His vineyard. We did have my son and his family staying in Italy at that time, so it made a huge difference to us feeling a little more at home in a strange land.

A local church in South Africa heard about us going to Italy, and we discussed the possibility of starting up a church in Italy on their behalf. We held a few services in

Milan at a private business facility; however, only a handful of expats attended a few of the services. Unfortunately, after six months, the writing was on the wall that this was not going to be that easy, mostly because of the language barrier and other factors beyond our control, as we would only be sponsored for six months and our work visas were running out.

Strangely, our time spent in Italy was exactly what we needed at that point in our lives, and I believe it was not just the restoration we needed for our mind, soul, and spirit. But also to be a blessing to others in that corner of the vineyard, which the Lord had planned and certainly not us. The only door that opened once again was an opportunity back in South Africa.

Truly, Italy was the perfect place for the restoration of our downcast spirits after the collapse of our business in 2010.

On our return to South Africa, my wife and I secured work as lodge managers at different safari lodges near the famous Kruger National Park. This was another door amongst many that had opened, which we could not really understand, but in hindsight, once again, we were able to witness and minister to many people, whom we probably would have never met. I believe with all my heart that we were sent to these different areas to work because the Lord had a specific task for us to fulfil.

A regular visitor to my office at one of the safari lodges that my wife and I managed.

Another lodge we managed, with Aileen's artwork gracing the main gate.

A five-star safari lodge we managed.

The invaluable lessons that I personally have learned during these mostly difficult times, even as a child of God, are:

- When we pray and ask the Lord to open certain doors for us, He will open the doors that are best for us to go through at that specific point in time. However, this is often in conflict with the doors 'we think' are best for us to go through, and we get upset with the Lord saying that he is not hearing our prayers, and we usually end up 'kicking down doors' that were, in fact, closed. This is definitely to our own detriment, I believe. However, the Lord is gracious and, with love and care, brings us back to where we should have been in the first place.

- The Lord's timing is perfect, so firstly, don't doubt at all because the Lord has heard your cry and is busy answering. Try not to do it yourself. The Bible says in Isaiah 40:31:

> *They that wait on the Lord shall renew their strength; they shall mount up with wings as eagles; they shall run, and not be weary and they shall walk and not faint.*

If there is only one door (opportunity) open, which, in fact, you haven't given a second thought to, then many times it's probably the one to go through. Time and time again, this has been my experience and only in hindsight, as I look back, have I realised that our Lord's hand was indeed in every single one of those occasions.

The fact is, we had moved 20+ times in the 14 years since my business closed and during that time, we stayed in seven different provinces in South Africa and three towns in Italy. We were also involved in seven different churches across South Africa, one in Switzerland and another in Italy.

The comfort and spiritual enrichment that were brought to us by the people in these churches were incredible. Such wonderful children of God played an invaluable part in our recovery from the demise of our business and having lost all our earthly possessions.

These moves did, however, have a devastating effect on our family. Some of the negatives that emerged from our constant moving as doors would open and close were that my dearest wife went through a terrible and very sad time of depression, to the point where she no longer wanted to live. As children of the Lord, it was so difficult for us to understand what was happening to us. This is a real reality in the world in which we live. Circumstances can have an almost deadly effect on our mental state if we allow them.

Was there perhaps a conversation taking place in heaven as with Job in the Bible, when the Devil presented himself before God requesting permission to strip Job of everything. At the time, we did not know but could only see the futility of life and all the many hours we had put into creating a business from nothing.

My youngest daughter was taken out of school before her final year, thus not getting her matric certificate or even her much-anticipated end-of-year farewell function and of course for girls, that is also a 'big thing'.

Since the business collapsed, we have never owned our own home or vehicle again, and it was also not easy to find a church with each move, as some areas we stayed in were in wildlife conservation areas, where we were managing safari lodges, and it could take you up to an hour to get to the main gate of the reserve from the lodge, that is if a herd of elephants did not block the main gravel road to the gate. Then you still had at least a one-hour ride to the nearest town. Weekends were normally busy looking after clients, so a Sunday morning was totally out of the question.

At each lodge where we worked, we did, however see (in hindsight) the Lord's hand in our move. In one case, one of the cleaning ladies who worked for us stayed in a small town nearby. The first time I took her home for her week off, I found myself in tears, as she was staying in a tiny tin shed with no electricity and a 'long drop' toilet outside. I remember her even giving me some spinach she was growing in her small garden, and on the way home, I wept like a child again and thanked the Lord for His great provision in my life. Even when we think we have little, we sometimes have more than many others in the world.

We were able to bless her with what the Lord had blessed us with, and more; we were able to share with her about Jesus and the love He has for each one of us. I know that on that day we will see her in His presence.

This was but one of the many times we had the opportunity to share the great love of the Lord with those who worked for us and those whose paths the Lord had caused us to cross.

I do believe with all my heart that you need to find a place of fellowship where you can be part of the body of Christ (a church). Not just going to church on Sunday mornings, but wherever possible, becoming part of a church community so you can make friends and be a friend to others in the church. Get involved in service in the church; no matter how humble it may be, you do it as unto the Lord and not unto men.

Our children have always been and still are such a blessing to us, together with their partners and, of course, our wonderful 12 grandchildren. We have had the opportunity over the years to spend some real quality time with each one of our grandchildren, with the oldest ones who are now in their 20s and the very youngest, who are between eight and two years old.

We strive to continue to encourage our children and grandchildren to love and serve the Lord with all their heart, soul, mind, and spirit. To enjoy life during the good times and to wait on the Lord during the dark and challenging times, to love your neighbour as yourself, and to never give up.

My wife and I have finally settled down, as my youngest daughter and her husband have built us a lovely flat on their property, and we have access to their second vehicle, for which we are so grateful.

The Lord has once again placed us in a church not too far from the house. We attend the services and home group, which we find is such a crucial part of being a Christian.

Approaching the age of 70 this year, I keep myself busy by working as a 'freelancer' when and where opportunity arises.

As a registered national tour guide, I offer my services, guiding both group and private tours through sub-Saharan Africa. I also consult with the tourism industry and have recently designed tours through Africa for a motorcycle touring company from Australia.

I am also a registered VIP close protection operator and assist a local company with bodyguard work. The Lord has blessed me with health and strength, and I rejoice in that I can still be active in this late part of my life, especially more so to do the Lord's work when and where required.

This year, November 2024, will be 49 years since that one unforgettable night in that small hostel room that the Lord Jesus met with me and changed my life. Thank you, Jesus! I will be forever grateful! It seems just like yesterday, as I can remember every moment of that miraculous day so well; it's still vivid in my memory and especially in my heart.

This photo taken of me in 2018 is a testimony to God's transformative and keeping power.

About my dad, he remarried two years after my mother passed away to a wonderful Christian lady who was a matron, theatre nurse and a lecturer who also trained nurses in Cape Town. She raised my youngest sister and brother from a very young age, continuing to encourage them in the ways of the Lord Jesus. She also played a big role in encouraging me when I returned home at my father's request to try and sort out my terrible life. However, sadly, after many years of marriage, she also passed away from cancer.

My dearest dad passed on to glory at the age of 85, having loved and outlived two wonderful Christian wives, both succumbing to cancer and ultimately death, yet he never ceased to give God the glory for all that he had.

In the eyes of the world, he had nothing, but in the eyes of an Almighty God, he had everything, including a legacy he left us as children, grandchildren and great-grandchildren.

My dad and stepmother with my son and two daughters. The year is 1996 (so glad Dad was able to meet my family).

There was also a full reconciliation between my dad and me. He was overjoyed when he received the news about my transformation. He was a little sceptical at first, I am sure, but on my first visit home, he mentioned that Jesus not only gave me a new heart but a new face as well.

My five siblings are all still alive, with my older sister and her husband still serving the Lord fervently. My twin brothers both committed their lives to Jesus many years ago after travelling a similar path of rebellion and sin.

Our younger sister and brother, who were both very young when our mother passed, are both serving the Lord together with their beautiful families.

In this final chapter, I can't help but reflect on the enduring impact of our parents' legacy and the ripple effect it has had on generations to come. Their selfless devotion to God and others continues to inspire us to live lives of purpose and meaning.

As we pass the torch to future generations, we carry forward the torch of faith and service to our Lord Jesus, ensuring that our family's legacy remains a beacon of hope in a world in urgent need of healing and deliverance.

As I reflect on the journey of faith chronicled in these pages, I am compelled to extend an invitation to those who may find themselves adrift in a sea of uncertainty. If you have ever felt as though your life lacks purpose or significance, I invite you to consider a meeting with this same Jesus who has transformed my own life.

I won't promise you a life devoid of challenges or pain, nor can I guarantee material wealth or worldly success. But what I can offer you is something far greater—a life infused with absolute meaning and purpose, anchored in a hope that transcends the boundaries of this earthly existence.

In the embrace of Jesus, you will find a loving companion for every valley, and a light to guide you through the darkest of moments. His love knows no bounds, reaching into the depths of despair and lifting you up with the promise of a future, not only in this life but also in the life hereafter.

So, if you're searching for something more, if you're yearning for a sense of belonging and fulfilment that eludes you, I urge you to open your heart to Jesus. For in Him, you will discover the true essence of life—forgiveness of sin, a life abundant with meaning, purpose, and everlasting love.

Looking back on my own journey of faith and the transformative power of an encounter with Jesus, I feel compelled to share some practical steps that have guided me along the way. If you're seeking to deepen your relationship with Him and find a church with fellow believers to walk alongside, consider the following:

1. *Prayerful seeking:* Begin by earnestly praying and asking Jesus to lead you to a church where you can serve and worship Him with all your heart. Trust that He will guide you to the right place and surround you with a supportive faith community.

2. *Engage with the members:* Once you've found a church that resonates with your spirit, actively participate in its life. Attend worship services regularly, join small groups and Bible studies, and get involved in ministries or service opportunities that align with your interests and gifts.

3. *Share your journey:* As you embark on this new chapter of your life, don't hesitate to share your experiences and testimony with others. Whether it's with friends, family, or fellow church members, sharing your story can inspire and encourage others who may be on a similar path of seeking and discovery.

4. *Immerse yourself in scripture:* Make reading the Bible a central part of your daily spiritual practice. Start with the gospels – Matthew, Mark, Luke, and John – to deepen your understanding of Jesus' life, teachings, and ministry. Then, explore other foundational texts like Romans, Acts, 1 Corinthians, and 2 Corinthians to gain insights into the early Christian community and the principles of Christian living.

5. *Embrace spiritual growth:* Approach your spiritual walk with an open heart and a willingness to learn and grow. Be patient as you navigate challenges and setbacks, and trust that the Lord Jesus is continually at work in your life, shaping you into the person He created you to be.

By taking these steps and committing to a life of prayer, involvement in the body of Christ (the church), and study of God's word, you'll lay a strong foundation for your faith journey and find fulfilment in walking in the light of His glorious word.

> *Study to show yourself approved unto God a workman that does not need to be ashamed rightly dividing the word of truth.*
> *(2 Timothy 2:15)*

As I reflect on my journey, I can't help but acknowledge those young people who have not given in to the fleeting pleasures of this evil world. I offer my admiration and respect. You possess a rare quality, one that seems increasingly scarce among today's youth.

I can't help but feel a twinge of envy, admiring the strength of character that guides your decisions. It's a reminder that true individuality is not found in following the crowd, but in embracing the unique path that God has laid before us.

Above: My beautiful family that the Lord has blessed me with. Each one means so much to me and even more so to our Almighty God. The three inserts are of those grandkids out of the 12 who were not at the event. The oldest grandson and then the two younger ones who were not yet born.

My beautiful wife and I with our three children.

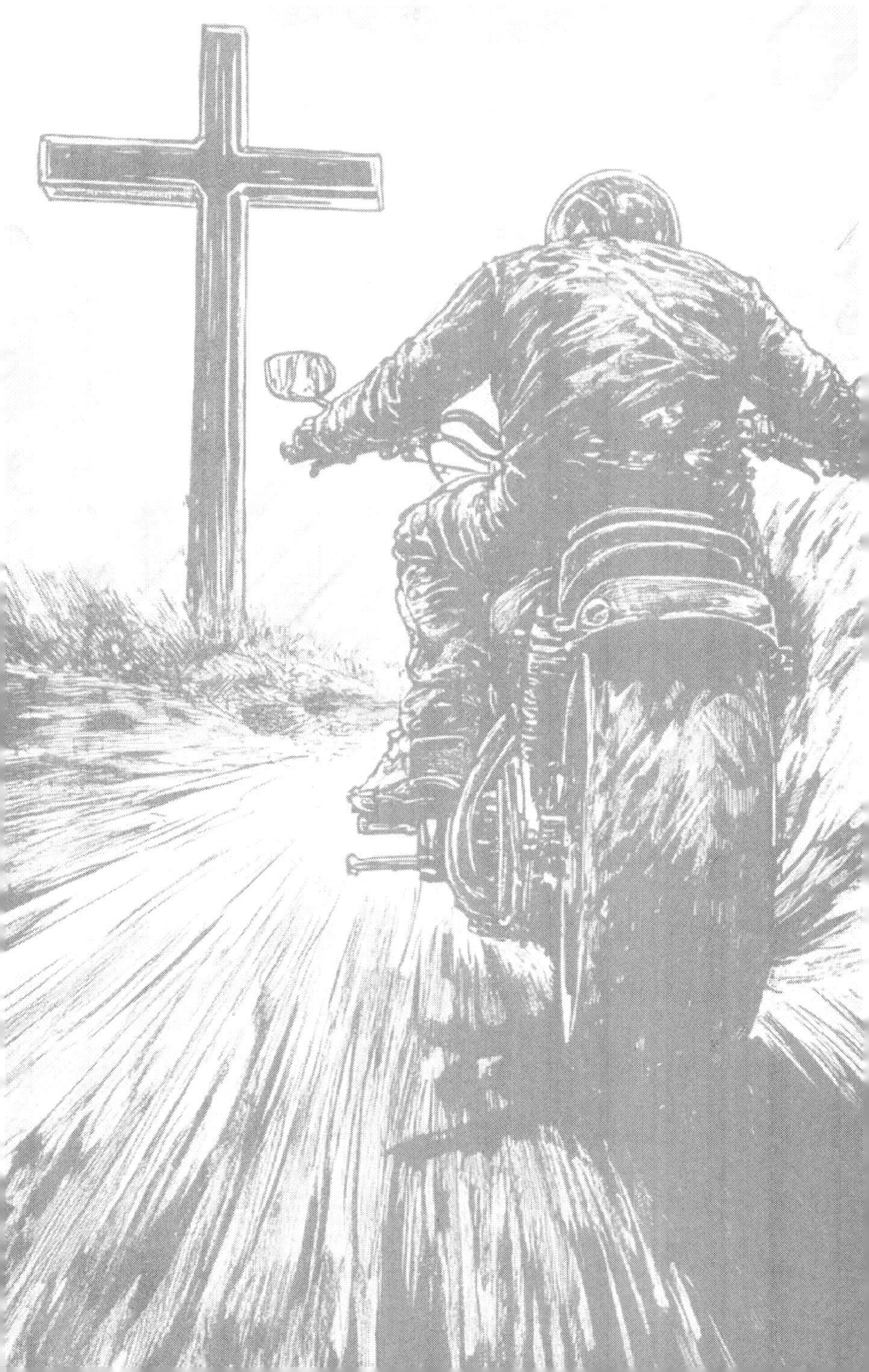

Printed in Great Britain
by Amazon